**The Parent-Centered
Early School**

Studies in Education and Culture
(Vol. 10)
Garland Reference Library of Social Science
(Vol. 1116)

Studies in Education and Culture

David M. Fetterman, Series Editor

The Parent-Centered Early School

Highland Community School of Milwaukee

Michael R. Williams

GARLAND PUBLISHING, INC.
New York & London
1997

Library of Congress Cataloging-in-Publication Data

Williams, Michael R., 1938–
        The parent-centered early school : Highland Community School
of Milwaukee / Michael R. Williams.
                p.   cm. — (Garland reference library of social
science ; vol. 1116. Studies in education and culture ; vol. 10)
        Includes bibliographical references (p.) and index.
        ISBN-0-8153-2399-9 (alk. paper)
        1. Early childhood education—Parent participation—Wisconsin—
Milwaukee—Case studies.   2. Education, Urban—Wisconsin—Milwaukee—Case studies.   3. School environment—Wisconsin—Milwaukee—Case studies.   4. Highland Community School (Milwaukee,
Wis.)   I. Title.   II. Series: Garland reference library of social
science ; v. 1116.   III. Series: Garland reference library of social science. Studies in education and culture ; vol. 10.
LB1139.35.P37W54   1997
372.21'09775'94—dc21   96-48330
                                                                                        CIP

Printed on acid-free, 250-year-life paper
Manufactured in the United States of America

Contents

List of Tables

Series Editor's Preface

This series of scholarly texts, monographs, and reference works is designed to illuminate and expand our understanding of education. The educational activity each volume examines may be formal or informal. It may function in an exotic and distant culture or right here in our own backyard. In each book, education is at once a reflection and a creator of culture.

One of the most important motifs sounding through the series is the authors' efforts to shed light on educational systems from the insider's viewpoint. The various works are typically grounded in a phenomenological conceptual framework. However, they will vary in their manifestation of this common bond. Some authors explicitly adopt anthropological methods and a cultural interpretation of events and circumstances observed in the field. Others adopt a more generic qualitative approach—mixing methods and methodologies. A few adhere to a traditional phenomenological philosophical orientation.

These books are windows into other lives and other cultures. As we view another culture, we see ourselves more clearly. As we view ourselves, we make the familiar strange and see our own distorted images all the more clearly. We hope this immersion and self-reflection will enhance compassion and understanding at home and abroad. An expression of a common human spirit, this series celebrates our diversity.

David M. Fetterman
Stanford University and
Sierra Nevada College

Introduction

The mission of Highland Community School is to provide a qual-
ity Montessori education and nurturing environment for eco-
nomically and culturally diverse groups of families on the West
Side; to be responsible for and involved in our children's educa-
tion; and to be a force for change in education and society.
                                    Mission Statement, 1992

In May, 1991, the newly chosen Milwaukee Public Schools Superintendent, Dr. Howard Fuller, visited Highland Community School.
His main question to parents and staff assembled to greet him was,
"What lessons can we public school people learn from you?" Highland people had cogent ideas to pass on to him. This book is a more
formal response in which I hope the hundreds of people who have
continuously created Highland in its first twenty-five years speak
through me in answer to him and to his colleagues elsewhere in
public education.

Highland began in late 1968, and by 1994 was one of only ten
schools in the entire country to qualify for state-financed vouchers
to independent urban schools. It is small: about seventy ethnically
and economically diverse students aged two-and-a-half to ten years,
three teachers and three assistants, a full-time executive director, and
three part-time helpers, including a parent coordinator. One of the
teachers doubles as principal. Annual expenditures per pupil are about
$2,800. The curriculum is Montessori-based. The building is a cen-
tury-old mansion. The school is governed by a nine-member parent
board of directors and helped, primarily in fund-raising, by an advisory group of trustees. It is located in Milwaukee's Near West Side,
an economically depressed and violent neighborhood (Jeffrey

Dahmer's apartment, since razed, was only five blocks from the school).

This is the story of a small school. Faced with the vastness of urban decay and its impact on educational institutions, the reader might question whether describing and analyzing this diminutive organization has any relevance to urban education. Despite differences between it and stereotypical urban public schools, however, it brings a message to American education much more important than its size seems to warrant.

Its size is precisely the point. Change nucleates and incubates in small settings. Our huge society conditions us to think in terms of large numbers, sweeping change, vast federal programs. Government may be able to create contexts for change, but the changes themselves have to be brought about where individuals assemble to meet their mutual needs. Whether their relationships will be harmonious and productive, or acrimonious and dysfunctional, depends on how the organization is structured and what spirit has been breathed into it.

This book fleshes out the organizational and attitudinal reasons that Highland works so well and what public education can learn from this small inner-city educational oasis. As a framework for the organization of this study, let us first review factors that research has revealed make a school effective.

Research on Characteristics of Effective Schools

What makes a school effective? Multitudes of studies have answered this question in a number of ways, and syntheses of these studies have appeared in recent years (Purkey, S., and Smith, M., 1983; "Effective Schooling Practices," 1990; *Why Do Some Urban Schools Succeed?*, 1980).

The Relationship Between Organizational and School Climate Variables

Purkey and Smith (1983) distinguished between "organizational/ structural variables" and "climate/process variables." The former are input factors that can be directly manipulated or acted upon in schools; the latter are outcomes, not subject to direct manipulation, which result when these factors are present. An example of an organizational variable might be a comprehensive program of parent involvement in the school; an example of a climate variable might be the sense of community within the school.

Some reformers took "effective schools research" to mean that if school personnel created certain organizational features in the school (inputs), "climate" variables (outputs)—such as a sense of loyalty, community, and empowerment—would develop in the school population. The connection between the two is not so linear, however. The relationship between what school leaders do and what they believe and value, their philosophy as it were, is mutually interactive. This book elaborates those organizational features central to Highland Community School which have produced its distinctive community atmosphere. But the study will also demonstrate that the school's organizational development has been driven all along by values and a clear sense of mission.

Organizational (Input) Variables

At the level of the *entire school*, instructional leadership, usually by the principal, is a key ingredient in making the school effective. Instructional leadership implies a clarity of mission, high expectations that all students will learn, monitoring of all staff efforts, and provision of resources to support those efforts. Autonomy at the building level for decision making by the professional educators is a second important feature. Third, staff makeup is stable, meaning there are no high transfer or layoff rates. Fourth, schoolwide staff development is promoted and is specifically focused in its objectives. Fifth, curricular goals are clearly stated and coherent, and the curriculum is organized and developmentally appropriate across the school. Sixth, successful urban schools, in particular, are marked by high levels of parental contact with the school and parental involvement in school activities. Finally, there is support at the district level for the school's efforts at change.

In the *classrooms* of the effective school, research tells us that teachers expect all students to learn and they interact with them positively. Their instruction is clear, focused, and appropriately challenging; their standards for behavior are explicit and their discipline is firm, fair, and consistent. There are opportunities for student responsibility, recognition of academic success, and minimal distraction from the academic tasks at hand. Homework is frequently given and closely monitored. Low-achieving, or "at risk," students receive the extra instruction they may need. And teachers employ a variety of individualized teaching strategies to meet the needs of each of their students.

Climate (Output) Variables

Chief among the "climate or process variables"—outcomes not subject to direct manipulation—is a sense of community within the effective school. Teachers feel a sense of efficacy and caring for students. Students also feel a sense of control over their lives and work and demonstrate it within an atmosphere of order and discipline. Teachers collaborate, adult relationships are collegial, and clear goals and high expectations are commonly shared. These climate variables are what I will call Highland's values and sense of mission. We now examine the relationship between organizational and climate variables as they operate at the school.

This study is organized so that the values which breathe life into the daily activities of Highlanders receive first analysis. The organizational variables follow. The reader should keep in mind at every point, however, that the values and behaviors of the people creating Highland are a seamless cloth. Neither is comprehensible without the other.

Chapter Overviews

The first chapter describes Highland's history, its neighborhood, measures of its students' success, and briefly, its people and programs. Highland exists in an extremely trying environment, not only due to neighborhood poverty and violence, but also due to its lack of access to financial resources. What Highland has done, therefore, may not be *exactly* what a school in a different urban context might try, but the similarities warrant close examination.

The fundamental feature of Highland is its purpose, a vision shared by all its participants. The mission statement, save the reference to Montessori, opening this introduction is one any public school could espouse, something that could not be said of effective Catholic or other religious schools (Bryk et al., 1993).

Central to Highland's vision is its active desire to include others who are economically and ethnically different. The school embodies the value of cultural diversity. Yet Highland calls itself a school which is a community. Community there seems built on intense participation and the more specific values of egalitarianism, child nurturance, and nonviolence as one parent was later to put it, "Highland is the world the way it should be." How these values intertwine at Highland are the subjects of chapters 2 and 3, respectively.

The school has developed a model parent involvement program that is a bedrock strategy, such that without parents functioning in every capacity and at all levels, the school would cease to exist. "Parents" means parents, of course, but it also refers to other adults who may not be official parents but who function as such. "Parent-centeredness" is such an important feature of Highland that three chapters are devoted to it.

Chapter 4 reviews research literature on three aspects of parental involvement in their children's education: (1) the effects of socioeconomic factors on parental involvement; (2) the effects of parental involvement on student achievement; and (3) the effects on student achievement of school programs designed to involve disadvantaged parents intensively. Its central conclusion is that what parents do at home with their children regarding school is the key. Schools can affect these parental behaviors by creating appropriate parent involvement programs. Chapter 5 discusses the practices and attitudes of current parents of Highland, with particular attention to how parents' involvement at school affects their interaction with their children. Chapter 6 focuses exclusively on parent involvement in Highland's school governance, an idea which is gaining some currency in big city public school experiments throughout the country.

Highland's trustees form a unique structural feature of the school. Since Highland's earliest years, individuals, mostly from the corporate world, have functioned as protectors of and advocates for the school. Chapter 7 outlines the history of this group and describes the results of a survey of current trustees' attitudes toward their involvement.

I have called Highland an "early school." By this I mean that its program is designed to educate a child for six years, beginning at age three and continuing through the equivalent of third grade, or about nine years of age. Although some Montessori schools in the country serve students of the same age range as Highland, the term "Montessori school" usually implies preschool only. Another reason for not emphasizing the term Montessori school is to call attention to the school's age-range (3–9 yrs.) which could be served by *any* coherent curriculum, not necessarily just Montessori. The early school's six-year program provides the continuous coherent intervention for disadvantaged learners suggested by research (Slavin, 1994a). Highland's Montessori curriculum provides clarity and coherence as well as proven "power" to the school's academic program. Chapter 8 explains the Montessori method, reviews research on Montessori programs, and describes Highland's classrooms and curriculum. "Montessori" refers to the philosophy and pedagogical practices of Maria Montessori, who established schools for slum children in Rome at the turn of the century. Her genius lay in creating an "environment" of self-instructional educational materials which the teacher, whom she saw as a guide or facilitator, introduced to the child. One of her fundamental contributions was that the teacher must be an astute observer of children, as she demonstrated herself to be in her extensive writings. The chapter closes by comparing Highland's approach to national school reform experiments, especially Howard Gardner's Project Spectrum and James Comer's school relationship-building process.

Chapter 9 summarizes the marks of Highland's success and, based on these, suggests answers to Superintendent Fuller's question, What can public education learn from Highland? The "parent-centered early school" concept is proposed as the next step beyond Head Start and Follow Through, the chief federal compensatory education programs of the past thirty years.

Procedures Used in This Case Study

Although I have been associated with Highland since 1969, and for five years had a significant hand in its origins, I did not begin this writing until 1989, after I had attended Highland's twentieth reunion. The reunion itself was the spark for this work. The spirit of harmony among the nearly two hundred people gathered from every ethnic and class enclave of our diverse society impressed me.

During the following five years, I made several extended trips to the school, interviewed several dozen parents, staff, and trustees, observed classrooms, and attended meetings of every type. Each data-gathering mission led to reformulations, although the ideas of intense parent involvement and the six-year early school curriculum remained as the book's main pillars. The research literature on effective schools helped me frame the structure of the book and gave me insights into specific questions as they arose. Finally, during a sabbatical semester in the fall of 1994, I conducted formal surveys of Highland's parents, parent directors, and trustees to add to the survey of former students carried out the previous year.

Although I wrote at the outset that those who have created Highland would speak through me, I know that in the end, I have only my own perspective. Where it is inaccurate, according to others' experience, I take responsibility. The substance of this book is others', however, and I am indebted to all those who have contributed to it. I wish to thank especially my partner in marriage of more than 27 years, Mary Alice, who gave me special support and encouragement during Highland's beginnings and who, through all our years together, has never failed to inspire me. Thanks also to our daughter Cara, for reminding us always that our efforts were for children, and who herself is on the verge of becoming a Montessori teacher. Those whose names appear do so with their permission, but there are many others not named who also built Highland. I am also indebted to several reviewers, including some at Highland and our older daughter, Christa, who spent her first year of school at Highland, for their excellent suggestions. I am further indebted to my editors at Garland Publishing, Marie Ellen Larcada, David Fetterman, and especially Carol Buell, whose insights made the book a better one. I dedicate this book, finally, to the people of Highland, who have with a mighty effort forged a space for their children and children to come where these young people are affirmed and strengthened to live in the future.

With these thoughts I now report to you the Highland Community School experience.

The Parent-Centered
Early School

Chapter One
Highland the School

Highland is the world the way it ought to be.

Johnny Kimble
Highland parent

This chapter introduces Highland Community School: its neighborhood location and history, its organizational structure and programs, milestones in its growth and development created by teachers and administrators, and measures of its effectiveness. We begin with a trip back to Highland's origins.

Highland's Origins
Highland's Immediate Neighborhood in 1969

Imagine that it is summer's end, 1969, and that we are on a helicopter flying at about 1,000 feet directly west from downtown Milwaukee, away from Lake Michigan. Just to our left is the campus of Marquette University, marching several blocks up Wisconsin Avenue, the street that divides the city into north and south. Highland Boulevard parallels it just four blocks to the north, forming the southern border of a patch of cleared land, interrupted only by an occasional tree, several blocks on a side.

The massive frame double-decker houses, erected by German immigrants before the turn of the century but worn out under rental pressure and absentee landlords, have been razed en masse. Although the federal government's approach during the previous two decades has been to tear down old inner-city housing and replace it with public housing, the only replacement in this area is a small two-story public housing project for low-income families and a tower for the elderly. Side by side they occupy only four square blocks, surrounded on three sides by vacant acres. State Street, just a block south of Highland, is Milwaukee's skid row.

On the northwest corner of Highland and 20th Street is a three-story, grey brick mansion, the future site of Highland Community School. One block west up Highland is the present site, the Highland Methodist Church. Both buildings are in the Midtown Conservation Project Area. The Kilbourntown-3 Urban Renewal Project, described in the previous paragraph, razed all but public buildings in its region. Since the Midtown Project seeks selective razing, to "create more green space," about one out of every three private dwellings will disappear in the next few years.

The church and the mansion seem to be on an invisible line running diagonally to the northwest from the southeast and separating the heavily black area to the northeast from the predominantly white area to the southwest. Other significant population elements include Marquette University students in rooming houses, "down and out" derelicts from State Street, a sizable number of Spanish-speaking families, and scattered Native American families. Within a year a few new middle-income–oriented medium-size houses, and one- and two-bedroom apartments will have replaced some of the houses torn down. Their occupants will be mostly black.

Middle-class homesteads, mostly white but some black, dot the area. Six Sisters of the Holy Cross of Merrill, Wisconsin, live in the mansion on the corner, but few members of the white congregation of the Methodist Church remain in the neighborhood. Yet despite the destruction of housing, this area of the Near West Side is still in 1969 the entry point for new immigrants to Milwaukee. It is still marked by considerable transience as newcomers climb the economic ladder made possible by Milwaukee's industrialized economy. Movement for many is into and out of this poor area, rather than from here to there within it, one step ahead of the landlords and bill collectors.

Organizational Roots of the School

Three seedling organizations originally formed a cluster out of which the school grew. They were Casa Maria, the Highland Community Center, and the Saturday Morning School, which later became known as the Highland Community School. Understanding these groups and the conflicts among them gives insight into the roots of Highland's values as well as its present programs.

Casa Maria

Just a few doors up a side street from the church, a young native Irishman and his family have recently taken up residence. Michael and Nettie Cullen and their children, Willie, Brennan, and Bridget, have transformed their home at 1131 North 21st Street into Casa Maria, a Catholic Worker House of Hospitality. Nightly, dozens of down-and-out men and a few women from State Street converge there for soup and bread, a welcoming handshake and a smile, more often than not a hug. Nettie cooks for them and cleans up; Michael serves them and tends the three children. Some of the visitors occasionally sleep the night there. Mike and Nettie emulate Dorothy Day, the New York City woman who gained national recognition for her self-sacrificing work among the city poor. She was guided by her radical interpretation of the Gospel, a radicalism deeply anti-militarist and anticapitalist.

The Cullen charisma is beginning to attract followers to the neighborhood, myself included, mostly long-haired, young, and countercultural in appearance. The older homeowners of the block view the nightly welcome they give to the street people as a rude invasion of their privacy. An older man who acts as their spokesperson has organized them into the Highland Block Club, a loosely knit group of white neighbors who resent the rapid transition occurring in the area and fear the decline of their property values. They have the ear of the local city alderman, who sees the Cullen activity as a cancer in the neighborhood.

The Highland Community Center

Back at the Methodist church, the resident-pastor-without-a-resident-congregation, who is white, is trying to establish a community center. He wants it to be governed by a board of local residents and to provide service programs for them and their neighbors. The Methodist Church has authorized him to use the church building in any way he sees fit, but the Church has supplied no funds to operate programs. Earlier in the summer of this year, 1969, he incorporated the new Highland Community Center, establishing a board of directors which consists of himself and five black mothers from the nearby housing project.

By the end of the summer of 1969 the Highland Community Center has become a nominal umbrella for three programs. The previous February Mike Cullen moved his meal program into the basement cafeteria of the community center. A young black VISTA trainer brought five young white VISTA volunteers from different parts of the U.S. to work for the Highland Community Center Board. They intend to develop Saturday morning babysitting and after-school tutoring for the project children. The third program is the nascent school, operating in a room on the church's first floor. The elements are now assembled for serious neighborhood conflict.

Highland Community School
The Highland Community School traces its point of origin to the previous December, 1968, when Mike Cullen persuaded Anne Nephew, a trained Montessori teacher, to set up her Montessori equipment in the church and run a Saturday morning class for a dozen three- to five-year-olds from the neighborhood, including her own two and the Cullens' three.

By the end of the following May, Anne, then pregnant and thinking her work for the year was finished, was ready to quit, until Mike asked her to meet with me and two recent college graduates attracted to his work at Casa Maria, Sara Spence and Joan Fleet. I had been through a year of considerable personal change, having taught in an inner-city public high school and then been let go due to lack of seniority, and having married. Mike Cullen encouraged us all to operate a daily preschool program out of the church during that summer. We did, taking care of fifteen children two and one-half hours each morning during June and July. Sara and I then took two weeks out for a crash training in using the Montessori materials.

We charged no fees for this summer program, true to the spirit of Casa Maria. The small expenses of travel to parks and the zoo, phone and mail we paid out of our pockets. Anne and I were supported by our long-suffering spouses; Sara and Joan lived off their meager savings and worked at part-time jobs.

Heading into the fall of 1969, Sara, Anne, and I decided to operate a full day care program in the church, under the prodding of the Highland Community Center Board. Only too soon, however, we were forced to scale back to a morning-only preschool session when it became painfully obvious that the parents who wanted full day care couldn't pay for it, and thus we couldn't staff it. Sara, moreover, could not continue to work for nothing, so my task became that of finding funds as well as administering the program, while Sara oversaw the teaching. Anne, who would leave in October to have her child, allowed us to continue using her materials until we could find the money to buy our own. Finding a trained Montessori teacher became a priority, as we muddled through the entire first year with the help of about a dozen volunteers, mostly Marquette students.

The First Conflicts

In retrospect, the obstacles facing us in building the school program were formidable; they were compounded by our entanglement with the Highland Community Center and Mike Cullen's meal program. Our own ignorance and lack of experience was a heavy ball and chain as well. Every one of us wished to help the community, but differing ideologies among us led to serious disagreements.

The Highland Community Center Board wanted to control all activities in the church. That was consistent with the VISTA trainer's black power agenda—that black people should control services within their own communities. But the problem for the board was that it did not control the meager funds coming either to the school or the meal program. Nonetheless, the board sought to exert control. By mid-December the board ordered the meal program out because it conflicted with nighttime tutoring, its workers left the kitchen area messy, and building and health inspectors had become more numerous than the cockroaches. But Cullen refused to vacate the premises, saying he must still feed the down-and-out people who came to him for help.

In the meantime Cullen had persuaded the Marquette University Student Government to contribute the proceeds from a fast (one skipped meal a month) in the residence halls to the school. But the student government designated the Highland Community Center as the legal recipient. Projected first-year income from the fast was about $4,000. The Center's board president wanted to spend half of

it on pool tables for nighttime teen recreation. I wanted the money
to pay staff and buy Montessori materials. Thinking the school would
have to split these and other potential funds with the board, and
fearing that on its own the Center board could not generate enough
funds to meet the needs of all three programs, I began to move toward separate incorporation of the school. The five white VISTAs
not from the area, unfamiliar with the neighborhood and plagued
by their own personal problems, had become discouraged and quit.
The pastor, perhaps suspecting that the Highland Community Center
might not be viable, sided with Cullen and me. The president of the
Community Center board, in her frustration, accused us all of selling out the board. Aggravating all this were the growing demands by
the building inspectors for major renovations in the church building, which could not possibly be paid for.

By the end of the first school year (1969–70), the white pro-
tagonists, more numerous and more directly connected to funding
sources, had their way. A quarter century later, both the school and
the meal program continue on, although in other buildings. By Janu-
ary, 1970, the building inspectors were making moves to close the
Highland Methodist Church. In February it was shut down for vio-
lating a zoning ordinance. The evidence that the building was used
for an unzoned program was a letter I wrote several months earlier
to the alderman asking the city to build a playground for the school.

The school moved to its present location in the large brick house
a month before the end of 1969, occupying the six rooms of the
second floor. The board president dissolved the Highland Community Center corporation in protest against the "theological fascism"
of the Casa community. This rift got several days' worth of stories in
the local newspapers. It revealed the depth of the gulf between even
well-intentioned blacks and whites, originally attempting to work
together.

The Present School Site

The present location of the school is a former Victor Schlitz home,
of the Schlitz brewing family, built in 1890. Designed by Charles
Gombert, architect of Milwaukee's famous North Point Water Tower,
many of its original features remain. They include Queen Anne style
woodwork, the original all-wood surfaced foyer, ornate fireplaces,

stained glass, and a grand stairway. The house had been bought by the Archdiocese of Milwaukee and deeded over to the Holy Cross Sisters of Merrill, Wisconsin, for use as a convent. Remodeled to accommodate twenty-five sisters, it had only six in residence when they invited the school to occupy the second floor. Since we needed a day care center license—most of the children are still under six years old—once the school had moved in, the building immediately began eating up money for licensing modifications.

Robert Weyerhaeuser, the school's principal benefactor for twenty-two years, contributed the $12,500 necessary to purchase the building from the sisters in the late 1970s. Major improvements since then have been few, although the basement of the building was remodeled into a cafeteria and school kitchen. The Ronald McDonald Foundation contributed $43,000 in the early 1990s to build a magnificent playground in the side yard, which is now an attraction to children from many blocks away.

Postscripts on the First Year

Mike Cullen, anguished by the Vietnam War, joined thirteen other men, mostly clerics from different Christian faiths, who became known as the "Milwaukee 14" after they broke into the offices of the Selective Service in September of 1968. They hauled 20,000 draft files in canvas bags onto Brumder Square just outside the offices, dumped homemade napalm on them and set them ablaze, and waited to be arrested. This action was their statement against the war. All were subsequently tried, convicted, and served prison terms of one to two years. After his incarceration, Mike was deported to Ireland, where he lived with his growing family until 1991, when he was allowed to return to live in the United States, resettling in Milwaukee.

Mike Cullen served as the first "protector" of the school that initial year, chiefly in raising funds and finding helpers. But as he became preoccupied with his trial, his efforts, of necessity, faded, and others had to step forward.

A public school teacher was one of those attracted to Milwaukee from her home in rural Michigan by Cullen's work and the reputation of civil rights priest Fr. James Groppi, a white diocesan priest who gained national attention by leading blacks on open housing marches into Milwaukee's white South Side, precipitating riots. A certified teacher with a master's degree in special education, she gave us expertise and directed the volunteers from Marquette University, who gave what hours they could. She and Sara each received the princely sum of $200 a month for their labors. One day in February, 1970, she asked for a "personal day" to participate in a welfare rights demonstration. She was arrested for breaking a window that day and never returned to work, having been diverted into more radical activities. But she had given us three months of structured care for the children which bridged our move from the church to the convent-mansion. Anne Nephew had left to have her baby; Sara and I stayed on; and another volunteer fresh out of Barat College in Chicago and also drawn by Cullen, promised to return to work in the fall of 1970. I was able to get the two of them scholarships to do graduate work in Montessori teaching techniques at Xavier University in Cincinnati that summer.

Since only two sisters would have remained in the building the following year (fall, 1970), they moved out into an apartment, and Mary Alice, pregnant with our first daughter, Christa, and I moved in. We lived on the third floor for the next four years. It has been occupied by caretaker families ever since.

By the fall of 1970, one year after having started full-time operation and less than two years from its very origins, the school had taken on most of the outward shape it presents today. What remained to grow during the ensuing years was the much less visible but much more important network of "mature community" and focused mission that this book is about.

Demographics of Highland's Neighborhood, Two Decades On

The Near West Side of Milwaukee, Highland's "primary" neighborhood for admissions purposes, covers the region between 35th Street on the west, the I-43 freeway on the east, the I-94 freeway on the south, and North Avenue on the north, about a mile or so in all four directions. The Neighborhood Data Center of Milwaukee Associates in Urban Development (M.A.U.D.) compiled a profile of the service area of Highland Community School, one of their member agencies, in 1993. Table 1.1 compares ethnic/racial groups in the

Near West Side with the city and county of Milwaukee and the state of Wisconsin.

Highland's attendance area is the poorest urban area in the State of Wisconsin by several measures. By the 1990 census, the percentage of households below the poverty level was 53.1 for the area, compared with 22.2 for the city and 10.6 for the state. Only 37 percent of its families were headed by two parents, according to the 1990 census, compared with 57 percent in the city of Milwaukee, and 81 percent in the state. Conversely, female-headed households were 62 percent of all households on the Near West Side, 40 percent for the city, and 15 percent for the state.

Highland's attendance area contains a much higher proportion of rental units than the city of Milwaukee in its entirety. Seventy-nine percent of all housing units on the Near West Side are rental, compared with 52 percent for the entire city of Milwaukee. It is not surprising, therefore, that the Highland area has the highest transiency rates in the metropolitan area (i.e., the highest percentages of those "not in Wisconsin five years ago" and the lowest percentages of those "in the same house as five years ago").

Forty-two percent of the Highland area population over 25 years old has not graduated from high school. The city's rate is 28 percent; the state's is 14 percent. The unemployment rate in the Highland area in 1990 was 17.6 percent, compared to the city's 8.7 percent and the state's 5.2 percent.

Table 1.1 Ethnic/Racial Groupings of Highland's Area (by percent)

	Near West Side	City	County	State
White	37	71	80	94
Black	54	25	16	4
Indian	1	1	1	1
Asian	4	1	1	1
Other	2	2	2	1
Hispanic	5	4	3	1

Data taken from *Demographics of Highland Community School Service Area*, a Report Prepared by Milwaukee Associates in Urban Development Neighborhood Data Center, 1992.

Note: Column totals do not equal 100% because Hispanic is not a racial category, i.e., some of the White, Black, and Other categories are also Hispanic.)

Violent crime rates in the city of Milwaukee have been the highest along the North 27th Street corridor, which includes Highland Community School, for several years. Jeffrey Dahmer lived in this corridor. There he had found an urban setting where violence was commonplace and where fear made anonymity easy and victims plentiful.

The Current Highland Program

In the 1994–95 school year Highland Community School enrolled a total of 68 children, 43 in the Children's House (a morning preschool program for three- to five-year-olds) (with an Extended Day program Monday through Thursday for 13 five-year-olds) and 25 in the Junior Level (grades 1–3 grouped together). An After School Program cares for the children of those parents who work or go to school. Most of the 55 families nurturing these children lived within a radius of three-fourths of a mile. Twenty-eight, or slightly more than 50 percent, of these families had only one parent. Forty percent (27) of the students were Euro-American, 52 percent (35) were African American. Eight percent (6) were Hispanic American. For the first time in several years the school enrolled no Asian American or Native American children. Thirty of the students were male, 38 female.

This racial/ethnic mix is deliberate. Highland works very hard to attract and hold as diverse a student and parent body as it can, given the constraints of receiving some public funds from Wisconsin's Parental Choice Program. Students funded by Parental Choice must be randomly chosen from the pool of applicants. Thirty (44 percent) of Highland's students qualify under State of Wisconsin guidelines for free (28) or reduced price (2) lunch (cooked on the premises). Highland is accredited by the Wisconsin Department of Instruction and the National Montessori Association and is a licensed day care center.

The previous year (1993–94) Highland's parents provided 3,465 volunteer hours, averaging about 43 hours per parent per year, the equivalent of two full-time staff positions. Highland's 1993–94 twelve-month cash flow report revealed that tuition income was only $35,610 (about 13 percent of all income), but that parents raised an additional $42,888 by donating further amounts themselves, supervising weekly bingo games run in concert with other independent schools and private agencies, sending out solicitations and running other fund-raisers throughout the year. Tuition is from $6 to $382 per month over ten months, according to parents' ability to pay. Tuition income has hovered at about 15 percent of all revenues for most of Highland's 25 years.

Total income for 1993–94 was nearly $270,000. Other sources of income included the trustees, who that year generated $105,671, mostly from foundations and corporations in the Milwaukee area. Two sources of income were unique: Parental Choice and AChoice. Parental Choice, the State of Wisconsin's controversial program to provide vouchers for elementary-level students attending 10 private, nonreligious schools in Milwaukee's inner city, sent $33,463 to Highland. AChoice, a kind of alternative United Way, sent $11,748 to Highland, one of its members.

The school is governed by a nine-parent board of directors, elected for three-year staggered terms by the parent body. All parents serve on committees, assist in the classroom, make instructional materials, and do office work, maintenance, and repairs. They also attend "parenting workshops" and parent-teacher meetings.

The trustees are an advisory group of citizens from the larger Milwaukee community appointed by the parent board of directors to assist the school in fund-raising and to provide legal, accounting, and public relations services. The number of active trustees has typically remained at about a dozen. Trustees have no formal authority over the school, but their support of the school is essential to its existence.

Key Staff and Faculty Throughout Highland's History

This section presents Highland's stages of growth as its people struggled to give it form. Although the focus is on staff members and teachers, most of the staff have also been parents of children in the school. Categories at Highland continually overlap and blend. That is one of its great strengths.

Montessorians and non-Montessorians

Montessori training for Highland's teachers has always been important at Highland, but even more important have been the values of the people who taught. Consequently, throughout Highland's history when they could not hire Montessori-trained teachers, the parents have hired teachers who shared Highland's values and were not already trained in the Montessori method, but who decided to become trained as they saw the validity of the curriculum by working in it alongside Montessori teachers.

Montessori-trained teachers in the Children's House in chronological order were Anne Nephew (1968–70), Talila Eyman (1970–72), Tim Souers (1972–76, 1982–present), Joen Bettmann (1976–84), Vicki Jackson (1984–1991), Maribeth Pinkerton (1991–present). All but Joen have sent their children to Highland, sometimes while they were staff members, sometimes afterward. Talila was Highland's first *paid* Montessori teacher. Tim Souers, after teaching half-time for four years, left to be the curriculum coordinator for the new Milwaukee Public Schools' magnet Montessori program at MacDowell School (three blocks down Highland Boulevard), then to serve as principal for the Milwaukee Montessori School. He returned to teach at Highland in 1982 and remains there, one of the long-term influential figures in the school's history. All three of his children attended Highland. Joen Bettman is now a teacher trainer at the international Montessori (AMI) training program in Cleveland. Vicki Jackson was Highland's first African American Montessori teacher.

Montessori-trained teachers at the Junior Level have been fewer for several reasons. First, for most of its history Highland has run two Children's House classrooms but only one Junior Level. Second, the Junior Level did not become a Montessori program until 1974, when Anne Byrnes, trained in the elementary Montessori method, began at Highland. Third, Highland's pay scale has never been able to compete with other schools for Montessori-certified elementary teachers, and occasionally Highland has had to hire untrained teachers at the Junior Level.

The elementary program began in 1971 under an uncertified teacher, Sara Spence, who taught in it for two years. A state-certified teacher took it over for the following year until Anne Byrnes was hired. Anne remained three years, and was replaced by Carol Hicks, another Montessori elementary teacher, who left in 1985. At this time the parents were unable to hire another Montessori elementary teacher to replace her, so they hired Paige Prillaman, a state-certified teacher who took the training the next year and received her

Montessori elementary certificate. Paige taught until 1992, when she left and was replaced by Mary Ann Erdtmann, the current teacher.

Assistant teachers have traditionally had considerable influence in constructing the curriculum, especially in the earlier years as it was being developed. For example, Sue Mroczynski, an assistant to Talila and formerly a Sister who had lived in the house when it was a convent, also assisted Tim Souers and Sara Spence in their classrooms for several years. She contributed significantly to the creation of the curriculum, as did Sara herself, even though neither of them were Montessori-trained.

Many of those who were assistants went on to become formally trained Montessorians themselves. In fact, as of 1995 all but one of Tim's assistants, most of whom were parents of children at Highland, have gone on to take Montessori training. Tim Duax, a former volunteer in Snoopy's Club, an after-school tutoring program sponsored by the Holy Cross Sisters, assisted in the Junior Level while I was administrator (1969–74). He later earned his Montessori certificate, taught at MacDowell Magnet Montessori for a number of years, then pursued and completed a doctorate in urban education. He owned a home in the neighborhood until 1992, when he moved his family to Shaker Heights, Ohio, to become the principal of the oldest Montessori school in the United States. Kathy Hubing, Tim's spouse, who was president of Highland's Board of Directors from 1989 to 1991, became a Montessori teacher herself in Cleveland. They returned to their roots in 1994, however, and enrolled their youngest child at Highland. Millie Deanes, the first African American to teach at Highland, was a national VISTA volunteer from Baltimore. She lived with our family and worked at the school for a year in 1973–74. Now Montessori-certified, she teaches at a Montessori school in Georgia. Mary Pat Rose, a parent hired in 1973 to assist Tim Souers in the morning preschool, stayed on for six years before taking the training and becoming a teacher in Milwaukee Public School's Greenfield Magnet Montessori School.

Administrators

As central figures will, administrators have lent a personality to the school from the beginning. (As of 1994, the title "administrator" changed to "executive director.") I was the first, serving for the five years from 1969 to 1974. The structure of parent power on the Board of Directors that I suggested during my tenure has been retained and even strengthened. I was succeeded by Sara Spence, who was administrator for two years from 1974 to 1976, and she by Cathy Miller, administrator from 1976 to 1981, a parent who had assisted us in the office for the previous three years.

Under Ellen Pizer-Kupersmith, the administrator from 1981 to mid-1984, the trustees became the working group it remains today. Phyllis Kimble, a parent and paid office worker under both Cathy and Ellen, filled in for three months after Ellen Pizer-Kupersmith left.

With the hiring of Ev Glaspey, a parent, as administrator in 1984, the school's organizational structure began to change. Prior to this period, administrators were practically volunteers, hired part-time at very little pay (I took no pay for my first four years) to do an essentially full-time job. This condition could not have continued forever. Accordingly, Ev proposed an expanded role for the administrative office, including an administrator's salary comparable to the full-time pay of the teachers (at the time about $12,000), a move which raised teachers' hackles, since they had always been grossly underpaid in comparison with their public school counterparts. She also created a full-time office manager position in order to free the administrator for more fund-raising efforts. The budget that year took a tremendous increase of 50 percent, but fund-raising kept pace.

Though a number of interviewees recalled this period as the emergence of a more "businesslike" atmosphere in the school's operation, not all approved. The school's next administrator promptly contracted with a parent, Mary Louise Mussoline, to function as a fund-raising consultant, primarily to work with the trustees. There were now four administrative personnel in a school serving about sixty-five children: a full-time office manager, a part-time administrator, a part-time fund-raising consultant, and a part-time parent involvement coordinator (a position which was supported by a separate foundation grant).

By February, 1989, when Bob Desotelle was hired, the Board of Directors had decided to combine the fund-raising consultant position with the administrator position and pay a "living wage" of about

$25,000 to the administrator. When I left Highland in 1974, the school had about 45 students and a budget of about $35,000. By 1989 the school enrolled 60 students on a budget of about $150,000. Inflation accounted for some of the increase, but even now Highland staffers receive between half and two-thirds the salaries of their public school counterparts. Yet turnover among key staff is relatively low, an indicator of staff satisfaction.

Highland's Effectiveness: Academics, Students, Parents

What evidence is there that shows how well the school educates its students? The conventional measures are usually grades, scores on standardized tests, and teacher evaluations of student behavior. Less conventional measures look at student graduation rates, success in school later on, employment, and other real-life outcomes. Since Highland perceives itself as a community, its measures of success also include parent outcomes, such as involvement in school, gaining further schooling, and opening up new employment opportunities.

Academic Records and Standardized Tests

As a Montessori school (see chapter 8), Highland does not use conventional grading systems which utilize letters or numbers. Instead, teachers keep extensive records on each child's progress in the various curricular areas, from introduction through repetition to mastery. The six-year curriculum is structured to develop increasingly complex concepts. To move on to new materials, the child must have mastered the concepts contained in the preceding materials. The teacher judges whether the child has the cognitive basis to proceed and decides when to introduce new material to the child. In other words, as one Montessori teacher in the Milwaukee public system told me, if the child proceeds through the curriculum, the child has learned what the curriculum has been structured to teach. Highland's students do not all proceed at the same pace, of course, since that is a feature of the Montessori method. But by the end of the third year of Junior Level (the equivalent of third grade), virtually every student has achieved the minimum objectives set by the Milwaukee Public Schools.

The Iowa Test of Basic Skills given to third-year students shows

Highland students averaging between the 75th and 85th percentiles in math and reading each year, compared to the Milwaukee Public Schools students as a whole, who have averaged between the 55th and 60th percentiles. Highland's student population, demographically, is about the same as the Milwaukee Public Schools. An article in *The Milwaukee Sentinel* (Herzog, 1993) reported Highland's third-year students performing two years above grade level on the 1991–92 Iowa Test of Basic Skills.

Highland has also begun giving standardized tests to its five- and six-year-olds at the end of their Extended Day year, prior to entering the Junior Level. Table 1.2 shows the results of the Iowa Test of Basic Skills given to thirteen of these students at the end of the 1993–94 school year.

Table 1.2 Average Scores on ITBS for Extended Day Students by Race/Ethnicity, 1994

Race/Ethnicity	Math Percentile	(G.E.*)	Reading Percentile	(G.E.*)
African American	75th	(1.3)	70th	(1.6)
Hispanic	85th	(1.6)	70th	(1.6)
Euro-American	88th	(1.3)	79th	(1.8)
OVERALL	85th	(1.6)	72nd	(1.7)

*G.E. means "Grade Equivalent."

A Survey of Highland's Former Students

In 1993 Stephanie K. Moore, a senior at the University of Wisconsin-Oshkosh, studied the attitudes and achievements of Highland's former students as a research project. Drawing a random sample from the entire list of former students, she mailed out ninety-one survey forms, receiving thirty-eight in response. A former student is someone who attended Highland for at least a year, then left; a "graduate" is someone who finished the Junior Level program, probably (though not always) having spent the full six years at Highland.

The ages of the former students in the sample ranged from seven years to twenty-six years, with at least one person at each year of age, except fourteen and twenty-four years of age. The majority of respondents, however, were over eighteen. The most striking finding was that, of the twenty former students old enough to have graduated from high school, *all* had graduated (one received his GED). In addition, all twenty, averaging 21.6 years of age at the time of the survey, had done academic work beyond high school, averaging 2.7 years of enrollment in either college or technical school.

In the sample, 45 percent (17) identified themselves as African American, 45 percent (17) as Euro-American, and 10 percent (4) as Hispanic. Of those who graduated from high school, however, 75 percent (15) were Euro-American and 25 percent (5) were African American, which reflects the fact that in some of the earlier years of Highland, there were proportionately more Euro-Americans than African Americans.

In the set of questions requiring degrees of agreement or disagreement all but five strongly agreed that they still enjoyed learning; all but two strongly agreed that they enjoyed the Montessori method of learning. Only four of the thirty-eight thought that Montessori might have caused problems in their later school learning, although thirteen (34 percent) said they had some problems with the learning techniques of schools they attended after Highland.

Did Highland's former students have difficulty adjusting to their new schools? Fifty-five percent (21) said they had some degree of difficulty in making the transition from a smaller program where they could proceed at their own pace to larger classrooms where everyone moved in lockstep. In their written comments four former students suggested that Highland needed to prepare students better for this transition, although no specific suggestions were made. Highland has a policy that "homework" is largely confined to school hours, but is given to be done at home in the third year of the Junior Level. This change is made to help students through their transition from Highland to traditional schools.

Highland's former students showed evidence of high self-esteem. All but four said they strongly agreed with the statement, "I usually feel good about myself," and almost all rejected the statement, "I often do not feel confident." All but one either moderately or strongly agreed with, "I usually set goals for myself I can achieve."

Independence was measured by five questions, and again Highlanders gave indications that they were an independent lot. Most agreed they were more leaders than followers, that they were independent persons, and that they were usually not afraid to voice their opinions. The strongest agreement of all, however, was with the desire to travel to other countries, all but six strongly agreeing. Both wishing to travel to other countries and not fearing to voice one's opinion were significantly correlated. Perhaps the desire to travel is a by-product of Highland's culturally mixed student population.

As to the former students' sense of social responsibility, thirty-seven of thirty-eight strongly agreed with the statement, "I would like to help make the world a better place for all of us." And all but six strongly agreed with, "I tend to get involved with people who work toward positive goals."

In their written comments about Highland's strengths, the most frequent theme was that of a feeling of community. Highland, they said, projected a family feeling where children are given respect by all the adults and where "teachers treat children as people." The sub-theme of racial and ethnic harmony surfaced often. Said one: "I feel one of Highland's true strengths is the blending of race and socio-economic groups, coupled with treating all people with respect."

Many also said the curriculum was a strength. Students learned at their own pace in the "Montessori way." That is, "the students were given independence"; "the curriculum was open-minded and stimulating"; "the teachers didn't push too hard, but kept us going"; "they taught us about the environment and domestic life, as well as math, science, history, English and the basics." One student spoke of a "wonderful memory" of a teacher splitting open a coconut and letting each child drink some of its milk; another spoke of loving "the wide array of out-of-the-classroom escapades."

What areas of Highland did they think needed improvement? The need for more funding was mentioned explicitly by six, implicitly by several others in statements like, "more resources like art and music, things that cost money." Four mentioned the need to prepare students for transition to the next school; two said the program should be expanded; three said there should be even more parental involvement. A seven-year-old simply said, "the food."

Nearly 80 percent (30) said they would send their children to Highland, often indicating enthusiasm. Three said maybe, citing concerns about the further deterioration of the neighborhood. Of the four who said they wouldn't, one said she didn't plan on living in

Milwaukee, one thought Montessori wasn't best for children's creativity, and two others, including an eight-year-old, said they liked Highland but thought they could find a better school.

In summary, the survey of Highland's former students revealed that its students are very likely to graduate from high school and proceed on to higher education. The transition from Highland to traditional classrooms, however, was a bumpy one for many, but didn't make them swerve from their educational paths, despite their happy memories of days at Highland. Most of them said they had developed a desire to learn, a sense of self-confidence and independence, and a desire to explore other cultures. They also gave evidence of a sense of social responsibility. In their comments they focused on the school's "family feeling" and respect given to all there, especially children.

In the best of all possible research worlds, the sample would have been larger and even more randomized. The fact that respondents put their names on the survey raises the possibility that they might have been trying to say what they thought the reader might want to hear, that they are, for example, independent, self-confident, and socially responsible. (The design of the study anticipated this concern, however, by creating a number of question reversals, such as "I usually feel good about myself," then "I often do not feel confident.") A more thorough study, for instance, might have asked them to indicate organizations they have joined or activities they have engaged in which would fit a profile of "socially responsible." The strongest finding, therefore, is that everyone old enough to have graduated from high school has in fact done so; and virtually all of them have done a significant amount of post–high school academic work. It is obvious as well that the respondents harbor an affection for the school and that they did experience it as a community where they were respected as individuals.

Parent Outcomes

Several chapters are given over to examination of parent outcomes at Highland, particularly an investigation of the effects of their involvement at Highland on how they interact with their own children on educational matters. Suffice it to say here that many parents through the years have served as teacher assistants and have gone on to take Montessori training and become teachers themselves in other schools. Tim Souers told me that all his assistants have become Montessori teachers except one, who became a Milwaukee firefighter. Highland also keeps parents informed of employment opportunities through the use of a jobs bulletin board. Anecdotal evidence indicates that it is highly effective.

Summary

Highland Community School grew out of a Saturday morning program begun in December of 1968 as a response to the felt need of parents in its inner-city neighborhood for a quality educational alternative to public education in the area. The conflicts of that first year which led to Highland's incorporation as a nonprofit charitable organization mirrored the tensions being experienced in the country itself as it moved out of the decade of the 1960s.

Yet even as Highland has matured as a school, the crime in its attendance area has become increasingly more violent, and the residents' poverty has grown deeper and more isolated from mainstream society. Much of Highland's success has been not only to provide residents with a quality education for their children, but also to create an oasis of security and community within which they can build—and in some cases rebuild—their own lives. Teachers and administrators hired by the parents have, in most cases, themselves come from that parent body and have helped to form the avenue of leadership along which milestones in the school's growth have been placed.

That Highland is successful with its children can be shown in a variety of ways, from conventional test scores to less conventional indices of student success in later life, particularly the pursuit of higher education, development of cross-cultural awareness, and independence of thought. Highland is also successful with its parents, particularly in empowering them with regard to their children's education. The chapter shows that despite the worsening conditions of an already depressed area, individuals there can organize themselves into a powerful force against this decay and can create the conditions for viable community life.

The following two chapters explore the values and mission that infuse Highland's spirit. Chapter 2 examines the meaning of cultural diversity at Highland, focusing on its admissions policies and its multicultural curriculum. Chapter 3 analyzes the value of community at the school, which is the result of a desire to seek harmony within diversity, to nurture children as the first priority, to blur distinctions between roles in the school, and to promote nonviolence in a violent neighborhood and world.

Chapter Two
Cultural Diversity at Highland

We saw the elephants and the giraffes, but where were the Germans?

> *Four-year-old African American boy upon returning to Highland from a field trip to the Milwaukee Zoo*

The innocence of children, their wonderment at the human diversity of the world, is fertile soil for learning. Many Highland parents, whether minority or Caucasian, commented to me, during interviews between 1989 and 1994, that they wanted their children to learn that other kids were basically like themselves, but also that the cultural differences among them made each child special and worth getting to know. Some Highland adults mentioned that the children already had internalized this value, treating each other as equals. A survey of the parents during the 1994–95 school year showed that all but one of them chose Highland's cultural diversity as one of the reasons they sent their children there.

As America heads into a new millennium, it is becoming more culturally diverse than ever. In 1990 the population of the United States was 76% Anglo, 12% black, 9% Latino, and 3% Asian. By 2050 the breakdown is projected to be 52% Anglo, 16% black, 22% Latino, and 10% Asian ("The New Face of America," 1993). Schools will have much to do with how well Americans of the future live together as a nation.

This chapter examines how "cultural diversity" works at Highland Community School, especially as it pertains to harmonizing differing racial and ethnic identities, but the phrase also draws our attention to gender, economic, and ideological differences as well.

Highland Community School educates for cultural diversity, directly through its curriculum, less directly through its very organizational structures and operation. The school's recruitment and admissions policies, staffing, parent involvement, tuition schedules, decision-making structures, and ties with neighborhood institutions all reflect the basic ethos of the school—a welcoming openness to cultural, racial, gender, and socioeconomic differences. Although most of the chapter will concern multicultural issues in the curriculum, we begin with a discussion of Highland's admission policy, because it reveals the school's desire to be a multicultural community.

Highland's Admissions Policies

Highland is a small school and yearly receives far more applications than it can accept. Accordingly, the school has established a complex set of criteria for admission to its program. Some of these criteria are formally stated in writing; others operate informally.

Formal Criteria for Admission

Siblings of current students are given first priority over any new applicants. But Highland's attendance boundaries apply to all applicants. There are two sets of geographic boundaries, "primary" and "secondary." New applicants from within the primary boundaries, approximately a mile from the school in all directions, are given priority over those from farther away. Secondary boundaries extend the area about another mile north and west; they were created to accommodate the tendency for some families to migrate farther away, and, quite honestly, to open up the possibility for inclusion of more middle-income families. New applicants from beyond the secondary target area are given fourth priority.

Students are usually admitted first to the Children's House at age three; Junior Level (elementary program) students come mostly from there. But children from other Montessori preschool programs may also enter the Junior Level, although they are given second priority. Third priority at the Junior Level is given to other children. All admissions to the Junior Level, however, must be approved by all teachers and parents involved, that is, the principal, the Junior Level teacher and assistant, and parents on the Admissions Committee.

Highland's Admissions Committee determines openings in all

classrooms "with the goal of maintaining balance in terms of age, sex, race, and income," according to the Parent Handbook. The sibling and geographic priorities insure that Highland maintains its neighborhood character, which includes considerably more cultural and racial diversity than the city of Milwaukee as a whole. But the choice of its families is not a purely random process.

Informal Criteria for Admission

There are less formal but no less important criteria for differentiating among applicants during their admission interviews. First, those parents of students applying who present themselves as willing to work have an edge over those who do not. Second, those parents who show some understanding of the character of the school, that it is a success because of its struggles, have an advantage over those who do not. Bob Desotelle, the school's eighth administrator, called these "people with heart."

Third, although "balance" with regard to age, race, sex, and income is formally stated as a goal for the school, its practical meanings may not be so obvious. For example, Highland desires to recruit minority parents who can take on immediate leadership (see below). I also recall a conversation about cultural diversity at Highland with a former parent and chair of the parent Board of Directors, an African American of middle-class standing. We had heard from some staff members, as of 1990, that the percentage of African American students was approaching seventy, mostly the children of single mothers. The former chair hoped that trend would not continue. If it did, he felt Highland would lose something very important by becoming homogeneous in its parent and student population. In the following two years the Admissions Committee actively sought to enroll non–African American children, and over time the familiar student balance returned to about 40 percent each African American and Caucasian, with the remaining 20 percent Native American, Asian (especially Hmong refugees from the Vietnam War), and Mexican American.

Highland thus chooses its parents and students in ways similar to public magnet schools. Public magnet schools, if there are more applicants than places available, accept students on a first-come, first-served basis as long as they meet the schools' academic criteria and as long as enrolling them does not skew the schools' racial balance goals. This public school selection process is not completely random, either.

Is Highland, then, open to the charge leveled against parochial schools, that they can kick families out or choose not to enroll them at all? The answer is yes and no. Highland can ask families to leave the school and has done so on a few occasions in its long past, essentially because they did not contribute their fair share of effort to the enterprise. And of course the school does not and cannot accept every applicant. But Highland does not "cream" the best kids nor does it take only those from intact, middle-class oriented families; there is a deliberate attempt to include a balance not only among ethnic groups, but also those from nontraditionally structured and economically disadvantaged families.

Highland, therefore, chooses differently than mainstream, white, competitive America would choose. Many of the parents who have succeeded at Highland—those who have stayed on and contributed in various ways to the school—on the face of it, have not been attractive candidates for membership in a struggling little program. Some were addicted to drugs or otherwise steeped in the self-defeating, dependent attitudes that they had no gumption and no future, or that they were terrified for their children and looking for a savior. Yet as a result of their involvement, they have served as members of, even chaired, the parent Board of Directors. Some became assistant teachers. Others have gone back to school themselves.

Building heavy parental involvement in a school, however, requires a core of adults who form the foundation upon which that involvement can be built. The leadership development of former "client" parents, who had previously been moving in self-defeating directions but who found hope and support at the school, presumes that there are already adults in the school who can act as the supports upon whom those stressed by the neighborhood can lean while gaining confidence to participate. Hence, Highland is continually on the lookout for minority parents who can exert leadership immediately. Highland's choice of students is under governmental scrutiny, however, just as a public school's would be, since Highland receives funds from the state of Wisconsin's recently enacted Parental Choice Program. In 1993–94 Parental Choice sent $33,463 to the school, a seventh of its revenue.

The Milwaukee Parental Choice Program

A unique law passed the Wisconsin Legislature in 1991 which allowed participating private, nonsectarian schools in the city of Milwaukee to receive a subsidy from the state for enrolling eligible students from the inner city. The parents of these students must live in the city and have an income below 1.75 times the federal poverty level (or about $20,000 for a family of three at the time). For political reasons, overall participation in the program is limited to no more than 1.5 percent of the public school enrollment and to no more than 65 percent of the nonsectarian school's enrollment.

Students can attend grades K–12 and, after submitting their application to the school, are selected by an "at random process," although the school retains the final decision to accept the student chosen. A Pupil Assignment Council, composed of one representative from each participating school (in 1993–94 there were ten schools), makes recommendations to the participating schools on how to achieve a "balanced representation of pupils." In the 1993–94 school year Highland enrolled fourteen students under the parental choice plan, four of whom were half-time, for a full-time equivalent (FTE) number of twelve. In 1994–95, Highland increased that enrollment to nineteen students, seven of whom were half-time, for an FTE of 15$^{1}/_2$.

In sum Highland's admission policy shows the concern of its leaders for the maintenance of broad racial, cultural, economic, and gender diversity in its parent and student body. There is continual concern as well that the staff, the parent Board of Directors, and all committees and work groups represent that diversity. Since Highland is an educational institution, its curriculum has a special place in searching for an understanding of and promoting a respect for different others. But the curriculum is not a separate program. It is an outgrowth of and natural complement to the diversity-oriented structure of the school itself.

The following sections describe goals for a multicultural curriculum, suggest several stages in building such a curriculum, and show how Highland fits this framework. But a number of concerns regarding cultural diversity should be mentioned first.

Five Concerns in Educating for Cultural Diversity
1. Diversity Is a Source of Conflict

The first point to be made is that cultural diversity can be a source of considerable tension and conflict. For example, the overwhelming passage of Proposition 187 in California in November, 1994, in which illegal aliens are to be denied free schooling and nonemergency medical benefits among others, may be construed as an economic backlash. But the fact that most illegal aliens there are Mexican, and most Californians are not, should not be ignored. If disparate cultures are to live together cooperatively, the tensions among them must be addressed first.

2. It Is Impossible to Label Cultural Groups Precisely

Neither race, religion, values, nor geography are adequate features of ethnicity. One must pay close attention to the "tangible aspects of group life" (Kleg, 1993, p. 58), ranging from athletic events, bodily adornment, division of labor, etiquette, folklore, and food taboos through funeral rites, games, government, greetings, incest taboos, kin groups, language to law, marriage, music, mythology, property rights, status differentiation and sexual restrictions (Kleg, 1993).

It follows that, given these many tangibles, it is very difficult for the outside world to understand an ethnic group's worldview, and nearly impossible to adopt it. Therefore, cultural diversity is not only a basis for group conflict; ethnic groups tend to maintain themselves by a certain degree of ethnocentrism, wherein they use the standards of their own culture to evaluate the meanings of behaviors or customs of another culture. Despite these obstacles, however, I take the view that cultural pluralism, that is, that perspective by which any aspect of behavior or custom is best understood in the context of the culture of which it is a part, remains the ideal level of intercultural understanding.

3. "Ethnic Purity" or "Cultural Identity" Is an *Idea*

There are two subthemes here. First, this idea in our culture primarily focuses on race. Second, cultural identity as an idea is a part of a person's self-concept, but only a part.

The Idea of Race

The idea of race differences defines our American culture profoundly, more so than any other, even gender, according to Cornel West (1993, p. 3). In our society, to an extent unprecedented in the world, except perhaps in South Africa, one is made aware in a thousand ways, subtle and unsubtle, of one's race: one is white, not black; or one is black, not white. Most other societies acknowledge the varieties of racial blends, but not America. In this country if I am white, I have that in common with all other white people. It is this *idea* which is so destructive of attempts at intercultural understanding.

Novelist Charles Johnson, in a June 21, 1992, review in the *New York Times Book Review*, lauded Kwame Anthony Appiah, author of *In My Father's House: Africa in the Philosophy of Culture*, for trying to find a firmer basis for African identity than race:

Mr. Appiah's repeated denial that race is the unifying trait of the African diaspora, and his jettisoning of all attempts to find a universal characteristic defining 'black' people, doubtlessly will bother anyone who has a personal or professional investment in the idea of racial differences. Given today's race industry, we are talking about millions of individuals—politicians, preachers, professors and poets among them—who can no more budge from their belief in racial (and gender) differences than the Inquisition could give a fair hearing to Galileo. But Mr. Appiah offers a brilliant, and irrefutable, argument about postcolonialism in which he concludes, "We are all already contaminated by each other" [emphasis added] in a complex, interdependent human world that is ill-served, finally, by the dead-end effort of engaging in "the manufacture of Otherness." (p. 8)

"We are all already contaminated by each other" means not only that we share a common humanity, but literally that what appear to be "pure" bloodlines are not. The genes of the "races" have already been pooled. But even where genes may not have been pooled, we are all members of the global village. The mores of cultures have intermingled to an extent unprecedented in history thanks to technologies which put us in contact with each other so easily. And since Otherness is an idea, it is subject to change through education. The social sciences, in particular, have given us considerable objectivity in approaching intercultural differences.

Cultural Identity—Only One Layer of Personhood

Shirley Brice Heath and Milbrey W. McLaughlin (1993) studied young people's attitudes about their involvement in youth-based inner-city organizations. They found that "the young did not see ethnicity as the centrally important attribute of their own identity" (p. 24). Rather, the multiple dimensions of personhood result from the several contexts in which the young person moves: community, neighborhood, family, peer group, social institution, even labels of ethnic membership defined by the larger society. So someone might be simultaneously son, Latino, student, Baptist, fighter, athlete, immigrant, brother.

The youth programs that were successful with these inner-city youth struck a balance with regard to ethnic celebration and education. They paid attention to the culture and context of the young people, but they did not attempt "to herd them into ethnic membership as the single or primary key to self-identification." (Heath & McLaughlin, p. 222) These young persons' sense of self-worth came from being members of groups or teams noted for their accomplishment (dance groups or athletic teams); their sense of belonging came from being needed within the organization. The successful youth groups didn't try to control their behavior or label them as deviant or deficient. Instead they offered them opportunities for accomplishment and skill development, while holding high expectations for such achievement.

A further point in the Heath and McLaughlin study was that if a youth group did focus on ethnicity, the focus had to be based on the local context to be successful. For example, in a particular neighborhood where families were mixed, such as having members from Mexico, Puerto Rico, and South America (e.g., Peru), the youth resisted an emphasis on "Puerto Rico" only. Many saw these notions of "ethnic purity" or "cultural identity" as "anachronistic symbols of another generation and political agenda" (p. 222).

Although these were youth in their adolescence, the Heath and McLaughlin analysis applies to younger children by analogy. Young children are not building a self-identity in the same ways they will as teens, but it is safe to say that the identity they have built by early elementary age is multilayered. A successful school will address the issues of cultural diversity in an age-appropriate way, but it will not try to push the students into ethnic membership as the primary source of their identity. It will emphasize accomplishment and belonging as well as cultural background. It will celebrate ethnic backgrounds by exploring them respectfully.

Under some circumstances, however, programs designed exclusively for children of a perceived homogeneous cultural group may be appropriate. I am thinking specifically of schools for African American males and females. Such schools represent an extreme response to an extreme problem: the potential for young people to grow up in some urban neighborhoods without a sense of a future for themselves, with little idea of responsibility for the common good, without feelings that they matter at all. Carol Ascher (1992) gave a rationale for the common features of the twenty or so programs she investigated.

Ideally, the programs offer: 1) appropriate role models of the same sex and an opportunity for same-sex bonding; 2) help with the transition to manhood or womanhood through formalized male and female initiation rites; 3) cultural inoculation, which includes both a strand that develops identity and self-esteem and a strand that develops academic values and skills; 4) strengthened parent and community involvement; 5) a safe haven. (p. 779)

These programs, however, have been a source of considerable controversy within the African American community as well as outside it, and their short lives are still precarious. Ascher explains the idea of "cultural inoculation" as "a dose of African American history and an Afrocentric curriculum that includes a variety of African and African American cultural elements" intended to strengthen students' self-esteem and their academic values and skills. The few evaluative studies done have shown participants had increased school attendance, lower suspension rates, and higher grades. Ascher refers to anecdotal data which indicate diminished discipline problems and heightened self-esteem. Ascher's recommendation is that since public schools have so poorly served such students in the past, the emergence of these creative grass-roots alternatives should be allowed to flourish.

In summary, educational programs which introduce children to their cultural heritage do seem to help their self-esteem. But the positive influence of the programs also seems in direct proportion to how influential the adults running them are in the lives of these children and how sensitive the programs are to the context in which the children live.

4. Educating for Cultural Diversity Must Acknowledge "Histories of Oppression"

Throughout history, groups have dominated other groups, to take what is theirs, to subjugate them, to eradicate them. Psychological theories about our tendencies to polarize ourselves into competing groups are not a complete explanation of intergroup conflict. Economic and political reasons are also important. The configuration of cultural groups in the world too frequently conforms to a profile of haves and have-nots, who either wish to keep what they have gotten, get more, or get back what they have lost. Or worse, to take revenge. Cultural diversity is not only about different folkways and languages, it must also take into account political and economic inequalities.

Assimilation refers to the desire by one group to participate politically and economically in the benefits enjoyed by the dominant group or groups. Separatism is the desire for a group to go its own way economically and politically because it has been denied entry by the dominant group. Much of the current discussion about multicultural education oscillates between assimilation and separatism, and the struggle by outgroups (minorities) for political and economic acceptance while at the same time cherishing their own heritage.

Cultural harmonization begins—but does not end—with accurate understandings of the different experiences of the ingroups and the outgroups, principally rooted in the injustices done the outgroups. Since Caucasians and African Americans are profoundly polarized in the United States, I will discuss them as my principal example of a "history of oppression."

The Oppression of African Americans

In his autobiography, *Maggie's American Dream* (1988a), James Comer is at pains to show the differences between the Caucasian immigrants' experiences and African Americans' experiences in America. In Comer's summary, European immigrants arrived between 1815 and 1915, most after the Civil War ended in 1865. They settled in the big cities, in ethnic enclaves that gave them a sense of cultural continuity. These immigrants underwent three generations of development that paralleled three stages of economic change in this country. (1) They were uneducated and unskilled in an agricultural and early industrial stage up to 1900. (2) They became moderately skilled during the middle industrial period, 1900–40. (3) They emerged highly educated and skilled during the last stage of the industrial era, 1940–80. (A few African Americans, such as Comer's own family, fit this model. Comer's father, Hugh, worked in a steel mill; Comer is a college professor.)

But immigrants had the vote immediately and used it to acquire political, economic, and social power. And most gained higher economic status during a time that required less education and fewer social skills. Even in 1950 a man with an eighth-grade education could still support his family alone in a low-skilled job—rarely possible forty years later.

African Americans, Comer continues, however, experienced severe cultural discontinuity as a result of slavery. They effectively did not have the vote after slavery, and 90 percent of them were locked into the bottom of the job market. They did not have the same opportunities immigrants had. Still, even as recently as 1950, census figures showed only 22 percent of African American families were headed by single parents. Since 1950 economic changes demanding much greater education coupled with racist social policies led to "massive undereducation" of African Americans. Comer cites statistics showing how massively underfunded black schools were in comparison to white ones.

Education is increasingly the ticket to living-wage jobs. Lack of competitive education and omnipresent racism in society have kept

African Americans out of the primary job market (business). Hence the African American middle class is largely professional rather than from the business sector, and only recently from the government sector. In addition, some black families have been traumatized by the South-to-North and rural-to-urban dislocations forced on them, but Comer emphasizes that most black families are not so seriously disturbed, a conclusion buttressed by the extensive research of Andrew Billingsly (1992). However, the recent hypersegregation of urban ghettos, discussed below, has wrought havoc among the lowest income African American families.

Other Minorities and the History of U.S. Cities
The history of U.S. cities in this century has been rooted in the avoidance of some groups by other groups—of African Americans and other nonwhite minorities by whites, of poor people by middle-class people, of recent immigrants by those who had come before. The turn of the century saw a tidal wave of Eastern and Southern European immigrants move into the centers of U.S. cities and a subsequent movement away from them by the middle and upper classes established there. Most of the immigrants of the second half of this century, however, were not from across the ocean but from the former Southern plantations, Puerto Rico, Mexico, Appalachia, and American Indian reservations. More recently, Asians have joined them.

Other forces widened the divisions between groups. As the world economy became more competitive and computerized, working-class status became downgraded. The Vietnam War touched off a decline in traditional forms of patriotism. International events, such as protests against apartheid in South Africa, heightened ethnic and racial awareness. The American core culture began to seem out of focus, or at least less agreed-upon.

"White flight" reached a crescendo in the decades of the 1950s and 1960s as suburbs flourished at the end of new interstate highways slashed through old neighborhoods. It has continued to the point where by 1991 suburbs housed 46 percent of the U.S. population. The rate of suburbanization, however, is now greater for African Americans than for whites as the inner-city ghettos have become "hypersegregated" and ever poorer. Many African Americans are now returning to their Southern roots as well, because they perceive that the New South offers opportunity and a new life.

5. One's Cultural Identity Develops Through Stages

Educating for cultural diversity implies that as minority persons learn about the history of their people's oppression, they typically pass through a number of stages in their feelings about themselves and the majority culture (Tatum, 1992, p. 3). At the outset, for the minority person, say an African American, there may be denial of one's own heritage and refusal to accept one's own people. But movement into a second stage is typically precipitated by an event or events that force the individual to acknowledge the impact of racism on her life. The individual becomes aware that many whites will not accept her as an equal. This awareness forces her to focus on her identity as a member of a group targeted by racism.

In a third stage of cultural identity development the African American now wishes to surround herself with visible symbols of her racial identity while simultaneously avoiding the symbols of white identity. Immersion in blackness is accompanied by emergence of anger at whites. At stage four, now secure in her own blackness, there is less need to assert the "blacker than thou" attitude of the third stage. This is a positive stage of racial identity, which acknowledges there are white people who understand racial differences and accept them. A final stage emphasizes a commitment to the concerns of blacks, which is sustained over time. In short this view sees beyond blackness rather than mistaking blackness for the universe itself.

Despite the difficulties just mentioned, multicultural education must be undertaken. The next section outlines several goals for multicultural education, starting with the need to *value* educating for cultural diversity.

Goals for Multicultural Education

Roland Barth (1990) put the value of cultural diversity this way: "I would not want to leave a school characterized by a *profound respect for* and *encouragement* of diversity, where *important differences among children and adults* were *celebrated* rather than seen as problems to remedy." (pp. 9–10) In such a school there is an active reaching out to different others; but such reaching out assumes that this diversity already exists in the school. Valuing cultural diversity in a school is shown at the outset by welcoming culturally different others to participate in it. Given such diversity, however, how should it be used for educational purposes? The following are four suggested goals for multicultural education.

1. Schools Should Help Minority Children Assimilate

Quite simply, the adults in the school should strive to make the minority children and families feel welcomed and comfortable as full participants in the school's activities. Implicit in this goal is the assumption that minority students will make an effort to learn the mainstream culture of the school. Assimilation does *not* mean that minority students seek to become members of the majority culture, however (Breitborde, 1993, p. 8).

2. The School Should Plan to Help Majority Children Learn to Accept Minority Children

This goal implies that educators are responsible for acquiring knowledge of the cultures and languages of minority as well as of mainstream students and for using that knowledge to educate them. Teachers can gain knowledge of minority cultures through access to single-group cultural studies (Sleeter, 1993, p. 55).

Schools with representation by more than one cultural subgroup have an educational advantage ready at hand. Children are intrigued by differences and, given proper direction by teachers, will eagerly learn from different other children. For example, Daniel Corley (1989, p. 22) described how he integrated three hearing-impaired middle-class Caucasian children into his 95 percent African American inner-city independent middle school in Providence, Rhode Island. Despite his fears they would not be accepted, they were welcomed, their classmates learned sign language, and the older students demanded a course in sign language for the school. Diversity can be an educational tool.

This last example raises the point that while language is the lifeblood of culture, it is also the wall between cultures. Although it is hard to gain fluency in another language as an adult, some teachers have done so successfully. Some familiarity with a second language and culture, however, can be gained more readily by immersion in the language culture, either in the U.S. or in a foreign country. Chris Zajak, the teacher-protagonist of Tracy Kidder's *Among Schoolchildren* (1989), vacationed in Puerto Rico in order to gain a better understanding of the Puerto Rican students she taught in sixth grade in Holyoke, Massachusetts. Other teachers take training seminars geared to help them understand linguistic differences as well as other areas of cross-cultural understanding (Olsen & Mullen, 1991).

3. Teachers Must Pay Special Attention to Minority Students' "Histories of Oppression"

It is not enough to help the culturally different fit in, or to help everyone feel good about fitting them in. In the ideal school teachers would help students analyze, in age-appropriate ways, how inequality and oppression have created minority groups, while being cautious of the tendency for minority students, upon learning the details of their oppression, to either think of themselves solely as victims or to blame all the bumps they experience in life on oppression.

4. The Entire School Must Take Democracy and Equality Seriously

The school that takes equality seriously will help students develop their social and intellectual skills in order to take action on social justice issues. In the democratic school, teachers involve their students in issues in the community.

Stages in Developing a Multicultural Curriculum

Given the goals just outlined, what practical steps should a school take to implement a multicultural curriculum? Frances Kendall (1983) has suggested levels or stages by which to implement a multicultural curriculum; the chapter will compare these stages with Highland's approach.

Stage One: Implement a Social Skills Curriculum

Diversity issues should be handled in age-appropriate ways. For example, a three-year-old might use a racial slur toward another child, but because she can't yet take another's perspective, she would not fully understand that it hurts the other child. The teacher should say that it does hurt the other child, but should emphasize that "those words are not ok in this classroom." Younger children will respond more readily than older ones to such an authoritarian stand.

This vignette might occur at what Kendall labels the first level of involvement in multicultural education: implementing a social skills curriculum. We will see in chapter 4 how James Comer's model emphasizes this approach. Children need help learning to interact with one another, either inhibiting their own aggressions or standing up for themselves or both. Central to this process is understanding their own fears and discomfort with other children who appear different from themselves. Without discounting the "schoolyard bully" problem, many of children's hostile encounters with each other are rooted in gender, class, ethnic, or physical ability differences. "He can't play dolls with us; he's a boy," say three girls. "You talk funny," an African American child says to a Korean American classmate. "What's wrong with her voice?" says a classmate to a girl with a tracheotomy. The list is endless.

This level may stress tolerance, helping "different other children" to fit in, or developing good feelings among majority children about helping them fit in. These are necessary goals but not sufficient for full multicultural understanding. Following this advice, Louise Derman-Sparks (1989) adds two important ideas to the social skills curriculum. She insists that the teacher consciously confront stereotyping and the unfair behavior which follows it. And she would broaden the scope of the curriculum to include gender bias and discrimination against the physically disabled (the "differently abled").

Teachers should not ignore stereotyping and discrimination behaviors, Derman-Sparks contends, because they won't go away. Rather, teachers should act to reaffirm the limits they have set by not excusing these acts (not saying, for example, "Herman didn't mean it"), and by not allowing themselves to be immobilized by fear. Teachers should also show children ways to stand up for themselves, for example, by role-playing with an assistant or with puppets how to handle a peer who invades a child's space or hits: "No, that hurts. I don't like it. I'm angry! Stop now!" The children would then practice the role-play and discuss it afterward.

Stage Two: Enlarge Each Child's Cultural Knowledge Base

This domain of knowledge should include gender, class, and physical ability differences, as well as racial and ethinc differences. The challenge here is primarily to teachers. Not only must teachers learn much more about these areas, they must also confront their own biases ruthlessly, perhaps the most difficult of all tasks. Such a task cannot begin without commitment to immersion in the ways of the other. Teachers might live in the school's neighborhood, for example, or become involved in organizations oriented toward the needs of specific ethnic groups. Or they may simply read literature about and produced by such groups.

Stage Three: Integrate Multicultural Materials and Activities into the Regular Classroom

These may be activities which spring out of the children's expressed needs (see examples of such needs expressed a few paragraphs earlier). Or the teacher may develop the activities, such as a project to study neighborhood demographics or businesses (Sylvester, 1994, p. 311). Holidays are often the pegs on which to hang celebrations of differences (Christmas, Hanukkah, and Kwanzaa, for instance). Or a teacher may design an entire unit which affirms cultural diversity. Kendall (pp. 44–56) provides elaborate examples of units on families, neighborhood residents, ways in which we are all alike, or ways in which we are all different (e.g., work, eating, playing, living in housing, wearing clothes).

Stage Four: Design a Multicultural Curriculum Environment

Here the entire classroom and the year-round curriculum are all re-thought from a multicultural perspective. Kendall gives specific suggestions for language arts, social studies, block play, dramatic play, music and games, and cooking.

Stage Five: Seek to Change the Entire School Environment

This level results when several teachers who have been working individually in their own classrooms begin to collaborate.

Stage Six: Work for Social Justice

Teachers can engage in social activism with young children; according to Sleeter (1993, p. 57), they should. Perhaps an elaborated history of a cultural group's oppression is age-inappropriate, but awareness of these histories must inform teacher-student problem solving.

Derman-Sparks noted that activism may take place in the classroom or it may—perhaps should—include the community as well. She provides a sample case in which a white student persisted in calling a black student by a racial slur. The problem was solved by having a meeting with the offender and the six black students and two teachers who witnessed it. The seven black students convinced the white student it offended them and they didn't want to hear it again. In another vignette from Derman-Sparks, a teacher asked children who discovered the adhesive bandages they were using were called "flesh-colored" (i.e., white flesh color) to write the manufacturer and complain. This action led to changes by the manufacturer. Another teacher had the youngsters paint over a racial slur on a wall in the neighborhood.

The teacher's activism, however, should be reflective and at a "comfort level" the children can accept. Teachers should not foist their particular biases on children. Although teachers must teach from a set of values, they must be careful to allow the children to understand and accept the activity proposed. Since such activism may run afoul of parental concerns as well, teachers need to communicate their goals, engage in dialogue with parents, and be open to compromise when the controversy becomes too heated. In one example from the literature, a teacher who taught about Thanksgiving from the Native Americans' perspective angered several parents. But a subsequent meeting to discuss her reasons defused much of the animosity.

Highland's Multicultural Curriculum Compared to the Six Stages

It is helpful to understand Highland's approach to multicultural education by analyzing it according to the stages just presented. At the first stage, Highland pays close attention to social skill development throughout its programming, beginning with the youngest students and continuing through the Junior Level.

Highland's Social Skills Program

On an informal basis, Highland teachers are quick to catch bullying or intolerant behaviors children use against one another and use them to teach for tolerance. Examples are provided in chapter 8 on Highland's curriculum. The Montessori model itself also teaches respect for each child's space and privacy. Children's House teachers verbally correct inappropriate behavior in the group setting when it arises, but they may also utilize role-play if the occasion warrants, since group problem solving among very young children is not amenable to extended group discussion. The Junior Level students put on several plays a year for the benefit of the Children's House; these model appropriate social interaction as well.

Among the older students, including the five-year-old Extended Day students, social skills education is heavily programmed at Highland. In a 1994 interview, the Junior Level teacher, Mary Ann Erdtmann, listed several ways the Junior Level is proactive in resolving social conflicts among the children. The first is the explanation of classroom rules during the first week. These rules are few and stated positively, such as "Be caring to everyone. Clean up your environment. Touch someone else only with the person's permission." During that week each child signs an "I Care" contract with the teacher for the year, promising to obey the rules of the Junior Level, after having discussed them thoroughly in the group.

The second way the Junior Level teaches social skills utilizes the weekly Class Council. Every Thursday all the children in the Junior Level program meet to make decisions about interpersonal classroom conflicts that may have surfaced that week.

The third element in helping the children to get on well with each other, according to Mary Ann, is Tim Souers' "I Care Club," which meets every Friday and includes the Extended Day students. Using exercises from the student workbook, *Creative Conflict Solving for Kids, Grades 3–4*, written by Fran Schmidt and Alice Friedman (1991), Tim and the children discuss how to resolve hypothetical and actual conflicts from school or home settings.

The fourth element Mary Ann mentions is less specific but no less important: every adult working in the school knows every child and models cooperative working relationships.

There is a fifth element in teaching social skills, the "superhelper" program. The Junior Level children, particularly the second- and third-year students, can volunteer to mentor the Children's House children, acting as tutors or big brothers and sisters. Depending on their skill levels, they can also volunteer to help out in other areas of the school, such as the office or the kitchen.

Enlarging Teachers' (and Students') Cultural Knowledge Base

Throughout the school's history, most of its teachers, teaching assistants, and other staff have lived within the attendance area. Many of the staff have filled the dual role of parents with children in the school. They did not drive several miles from middle-class neighborhoods into unknown territory. In addition, according to Kathy Hubing, president of Highland's parent Board of Directors from 1989 to 1991, they have been involved in organizations working with local residents to improve neighborhood conditions. "Earlier parents," she said in 1989, "were connected to a variety of community organizations, such as Casa Maria, the Food Co-op, the Next Door Foundation (a youth service agency), the West Side Housing Co-op, Marquette Students for Social Action, Wisconsin Action Coalition. Although the staff seems more 'professionalized' and less involved now, there are more parents on the staff, and there are still all kinds of networks—neighborhood, political, social—that Highland plugs into." Pat Farrington, Parent Coordinator in 1994, pointed out that staff were still involved with most of the neighborhood organizations mentioned above and some newer ones as well.

Teachers and assistants continue to expand their cultural knowledge base more formally as well. For example, Eniola Oladeji, a former Highland parent and teaching assistant at both the Children's House and Junior Levels, has immersed herself in African culture and has become a leader at Highland in promoting cross-cultural awareness. In the spring, 1991, school newsletter, she wrote:

We learned songs, dances, language, dress, and foods from Yoruba, Nigeria. Onward to Brazil. . . . Our class visited the rain forest exhibit at the Milwaukee Public Museum, learned the Samba, and experienced a touch of "Carnival" Highland style. We plan on exploring the Hmong culture of Asia and the French culture before the end of this school year.

The very diversity of Highland's parent and student population itself is a spur to learning more about diverse cultures. Besides African American children present in the school there are, typically, Caucasians, Mexicans, Puerto Ricans, Native Americans, and Southeast Asians (Hmong).

Integration of Materials and Activities into a Multicultural School at Highland

The next three stages cannot be factored out at Highland; they intermingle and flow together. Each teacher's practice is planned in consultation with his or her colleagues within the overall goal that the school is to be a culturally diverse community. Though teachers may vary in what they emphasize in each individual classroom, they seek to integrate what they do with what the others are doing. An explicit example of such integrative planning in multicultural education is the choice of two different countries for thorough study each year.

In 1994 the countries selected for extended study were Uganda and Italy, Uganda being highlighted because of the negative images of Africa coming to the United States about Rwandan massacres. Previous countries have included Japan, Brazil, France, Nigeria, and Poland. Junior Level assistant Eniola Oladeji researches the dance and music portions of the multicultural curriculum, while Children's House teacher Maribeth Pinkerton focuses on the food. All the teachers take responsibility for learning and teaching some language from each culture. Other cultural aspects are brought into the school as available. For instance, Japanese visitors in 1993 showed the children how to do origami (paper-folding). The effects of their visit last year are evident throughout the school, including an elaborate origami globe on the principal's desk.

Highland's teachers tend to have strong ideological foundations, but they are not doctrinaire about them. For example, although Eniola strongly promotes non-Caucasian stories and themes, she acceded readily when a child asked that Cinderella be a production.

Working for Social Justice at Highland

Highland grew out of its founders' acute awareness of social injustices, a vision which continues to this day. We have already seen that

Highland's staff, and many of the parents, are involved in and knowl-edgeable about a wide variety of community organizations that are working for and with the neighborhood's residents. Just one example of how teachers take children into the field to teach for social justice is Tim Souers' yearly field trip to the Whooping Crane Peace Educa-tion Center near Baraboo, Wisconsin. There the nearly extinct birds are nurtured by a community of volunteers from countries around the world who introduce children not only to the wonders of the birds themselves, but also to the realities of intercultural conflicts across the globe. They seek to model how these conflicts can be overcome by cooperation in solving problems common to us all.

Summary

An examination of its admission policies found evidence that High-land values cultural diversity. These policies build the parent and student bodies to be as diverse as possible according to age, sex, race, and income. That cultural diversity is a primary value at the school is also demonstrated by the response of the parents surveyed. Al-most all parents listed cultural diversity as one of the reasons they sent their children to Highland.

Turning to curriculum as such, the chapter discussed five major concerns that educators must be aware of in multicultural educa-tion. Four goals and six stages in developing a multicultural curricu-lum formed the framework for analysis of Highland's educational program for cultural diversity. Highland has integrated these goals and stages into what may legitimately be said to be a culturally di-verse community, although its emphasis on cultural diversity is not separate from other community values. The next chapter analyzes these other values at Highland which help to meld its cultural diver-sity into community.

Chapter Three
The Meaning of Community at Highland

> *The biggest problem besetting schools is the primitive quality of human relationships among children, parents, teachers, and administrators. Many schools perpetuate infantilism.*
>
> *Roland Barth (1990), p. 36*

Community is an overworked word, but it still speaks to the deepest yearnings of the human heart. The Highland Community School *is* a community, but how it can be so while celebrating diversity is a paradox. I believe this paradox is resolved at the school by *not* focusing on community nearly as much as on cultural diversity. That is, at Highland the emphasis seems to be placed on relating to different others in harmonious ways despite potential conflicts, rather than on "we are all this way or that," which might be the case in another school trying to build a sense of community. This chapter elaborates on the other elements of Highland's vision of community: nurturance of children, egalitarianism, and nonviolence.

The Elements of Highland's Vision of Community

Highland people really value their cultural and other accidental differences. If they are all agreed on anything, it is this. Their mission seems almost to create a new world, given the diversity of the present one, within the microcosm of the school.

Thomas Sergiovanni (1994), a staunch promoter of community in schools, argues that a school community must first be purposeful, a network of shared ideologies, in order to give meaning to its educational strategies (p. 85). Highland's unique mission to build community within diversity rests on three explicit central values, all of which fly counter to current cultural value trends: (1) valuing children highly, (2) egalitarianism, and (3) nonviolence. Highland people know that underlying these values is the larger value that despite the individualism of our culture, we *are* our brothers' keepers. This sense of social responsibility gives shape and power to these explicit values. This chapter discusses the shared sense of social responsibility first as a prerequisite for understanding the rest. The chapter also discusses collegiality among the staff.

"At Highland We All Help Each Other"

Even Highland's emphasis on contributing to the good of the community is countercultural in modern-day America. It is worth dwelling for a moment on just how oriented toward the self our culture is.

Drawing on the results of a nationwide survey of contemporary American values, Robert Bellah and his associates (1985, p. 3) analyzed the shift from community orientation to self-orientation in American culture. They concluded that the great task in our modern individualistic culture is "finding ourselves" while simultaneously connecting with others. In our mobile, chaotic mass society, each of us faces the life task of gaining confidence in our abilities to relate to others without being overwhelmed by their demands.

There are still the cultural themes of yesteryear: the Puritan ideal of *community* (John Winthrop), the republican ideal of *political equality* for all (George Washington), the utilitarian goal of *material acquisition* (Benjamin Franklin), and the personalistic norm of *expressive individualism* (Walt Whitman). Yet all value-themes have undergone profound changes under the press of technological innovation, so that they now often contradict one another. For example, cultural diversity in mass society makes it difficult to relate to different others. The search for community in America conflicts with the just distribution of material resources, and there is little agreement on what just distribution means. Economic success goes at odds with achieving and contributing to community. Freedom produces isolation.

Finding Oneself

A rite of passage now at the core of our culture is *leaving home*, which in reality is a complicated process of separation and individuation. My mother and three siblings, for example, live in different cities in Michigan. My spouse and her six siblings are scattered even farther, from East Coast to West Coast. Extended families in close contact are rare, except among the poorest and the wealthiest. We nostalgically revere the value of "family," but the realities of modern life, including job moves, our career and other aspirations, and lack of institutional support encourage us to mitigate the real demands of family.

Another paradox in "finding oneself" is *leaving the church* as a near-universal requirement for self-realization. The phrase does not mean that all actually leave their churches, but that many now call into question their religious participation in order to either reaffirm it or let it go. Many reaffirm, but many others do not. Once again our culture drives us to define ourselves without providing secure clues from tradition to use.

A third way we try to find ourselves is in our *work*, so that many of us become what we do for a living. Upended by swift job changes or unemployment, those who identify themselves with their work face a deep identity crisis.

A fourth attempt at finding oneself is through expressive individualism (you are who you express yourself to be). These individuals create *lifestyle enclaves* as substitutes for communities. However, these enclaves are not really communities because they emphasize the pursuit of individual wants rather than opening the self to the demands of communal relationships. Current examples might be "yuppie up-scale apartment complexes," Sun City–style enclaves for the elderly, or "golf lifestyles," condos surrounding a course.

Connecting with Others

What of the traditional themes of connecting, such as love, marriage, and friendship? Even here there are significant cultural pitfalls, according to Bellah and his associates. Individualism says that commitment in a relationship must be preceded by one's own self-actualization. In a way, the basis for saying marriage should last has shifted from outside influences (e.g., Bible, culture, tradition) to inside: first become self-actualized, then you can love.

Erich Fromm, in his 1956 classic *The Art of Loving*, put the matter succinctly. Too many people imagine that love means a focus on making myself attractive, packaging myself so others will love me. Others think love means finding the right object to love, or on falling in love (the romantic feeling) instead of loving steadfastly (the act of continual commitment). All these errors, rooted in our culture of consumption, are self-oriented. Love relations now are expected to find their basis in *self*-fulfillment first, in the Bible, cultural traditions, or kin and the importance of family second.

This privatistic "me-first" attitude carries over into friendship and even into public policy. Herein lie the sources of confusion. On the one hand, we endlessly monitor our feelings and calculate the costs and benefits of our relationships. Yet on the other hand, life pulls us into risky, uncertain commitments which are promoted by tradition, especially marriage and civic involvement. If we avoid these commitments, we find ourselves unhappy. Yet their demands may upset our careful, selfish calculations.

In America the Self Takes Precedence

Individualism says the self is the main form of reality. Tradition says it is rather "the self-in-relation-to-others." The greatest irony is that in the contemporary United States both of these are emphasized more than in any other country: self-fulfillment on the one hand; volunteerism, charity, and civic involvement on the other. In our society, however, the self takes precedence.

This individualism too often shows itself both in private and in public as an avoidance of responsibility: parents don't want to know what their adolescents are up to; public officials don't want to rock the boat; citizens just want to "let someone else do it." "It ain't my job" seems the preeminent motto of our culture.

Beyond Tolerance

Bellah and his associates conclude that mere tolerance of differences among groups is not enough to solve our current social problems. There must be a concern which transcends protection of self-interest—for the common good, for the whole body politic, for the public welfare. There must be a vision of a debt to future generations that is not merely short term.

Highland has not been able to avoid altogether the contradictions of American culture. Although the school stresses openness to and acceptance of ethnic and economic differences, this desire for harmonious relationships has not precluded conflict. In recent years there have been serious disagreements over hiring and firing decisions, over distribution of resources among staff, over policies of admission and organizational structure. But adherence to the fundamental norm of staying connected, of valuing relationships with different others, has helped Highland weather these storms in its history that could have destroyed the school.

That Highland survived these and other conflicts demonstrates that the value of developing the self-in-relation-to-others, the value of connectedness, is a fundamental force in the school. Although the great divides of our culture between races and classes still affect the school, Highland continues to be infused with the values of prizing children, egalitarianism, and nonviolence.

Highland Values Children

The individualism of the contemporary United States militates against a public policy which would invest considerable resources in children. As a result, children, in a *public* sense, are not highly valued in America, despite the nurturance millions of parents provide their own children.

In the language of contemporary capitalism, children are items of private consumption. That is, the rearing of children is a private affair; government is not expected to offer much help. The result is that parents are expected to bear all or most of the costs of bringing a child to adulthood (which some economists have estimated at between $170,000 and $235,000 in 1991 dollars). Privately reared, however, the resulting citizen contributes to society in a variety of ways, that is, producing public benefits. All the parents can expect, however, is gratitude. The costs are private, the benefits public. But too many parents today either can't or won't bear these private costs.

This public devaluation of children as of 1993 has pushed one in every five children (22 percent) below the poverty line, and nearly one in every *two* (45.9 percent) African American children (Statistical Abstract of the United States, 1996, p. 480, Table 745). Poverty is the indirect reason 22.3 percent of all pregnant women and 36.1 percent of black women get little or no prenatal care (39.7 million Americans in 1993 had no health insurance). Their babies are forty times more likely to be born underweight and sickly, requiring costly care for years into the future. Four hundred dollars spent on prenatal care and education can save up to $300,000 on neonatal intensive care and tens of thousands of welfare dollars after that.

Public policy devaluing children shows itself not only in penny-pinching dollars for poor children; it shows itself also in laws and company practices which create stress in families of all classes and erode child nurturance (Hewlett, 1991, pp. 176–82). Studies (Haglund, 1992) suggest that parental time with children has declined ten to twelve hours per week in the past two decades, whether that be due to working longer hours to stay on top of increasingly precarious careers, or working to make ends meet, or just avoiding the kids. Whatever the causes—and they are several—the children suffer.

Half of all divorced fathers pay only partial (24 percent) or no child (25 percent) support (Statistical Abstract, 1996, p. 391, Table 616), and nearly half *never* see their children after divorce (Hewlett, 1991, p. 96). The average income of the men increases after divorce; but the women's income decreases—which hurts the children because the mother is ten times as likely to be the primary parent. In this climate of reduced supports for so many children, it is not surprising that suicide rates have for youths 15 to 24 years old tripled in three decades (Wright, 1995, p. 220), that half a million babies are born to unwed teens each year (Statistical Abstract, 1996, p. 73, Table 88), that adolescent emotional problems, eating disorders, academic failures, and criminal behavior have reached epidemic proportions.

Another indicator that our children are becoming less valued is the rise in child labor. The *New York Times* (Kolata, 1992) estimated that two million children under the age of 14 work illegally. Although no one knows exactly how many children work illegally, evidence from federal agencies, states' investigations, and emergency room records suggests that underage children work in fields, in the garment industry, in fast-food restaurants, on construction sites, and in mines, sawmills, and gas stations. On the job they suffer amputations, burns, deep cuts, and electrocutions. At least several hundred a year are killed.

The Executive Director of the National Child Labor Committee, Jeffrey Newman, said he is seeing a return of child labor scandals reminiscent of those that occurred at the turn of the century (Kolata, 1992). "It's very sad and it doesn't speak well to our understanding and commitment to children," he said. This rise in exploitation of children, he suggested, is due to more families slipping into poverty, immigrants from countries where child labor is routine, and cuts in government agencies that inspect workplaces.

This state of crisis for children exists because *as a society* we do not care for them enough. As I said at the beginning of this book, I suspect that broad social changes nucleate simultaneously in small settings where individuals congregate to meet their mutual needs. The increasing public neglect of our children is drawing attention and is being addressed in these small settings.

Highland represents one of those nucleation points for change, because it nurtures its children now and for their future. Over the years Highland has reworked the traditions of schooling by removing the negatives (school as a place, for example, where you *can't* do things) and by replacing them with positives. In the eyes of Highland's children, as we saw in the survey of former students, school is where you can learn about yourself and about other's worlds through experience, where you can build a dream, where you can be safe and laugh and talk and play and eat good food and have good playmates, where the adults, different as they may be from one another, all like you and talk to you—instead of threatening or yelling—and where you're likely to see your mom and dad, and they like it there, too.

Highland's Spirit of Egalitarianism

Egalitarianism at Highland blurs roles in the organization; no one's position is too important to exclude the most menial (though necessary) of labors. This spirit has lived on down through the years at Highland, prompted by a radical sense of democracy and chronic lack of funds, which requires that everyone pitch in whether it's their job or not. The following is an example of "radical" egalitarianism, which has changed somewhat since then.

Roles Are Blurred

In a memo dated November, 1986, Ev Glaspy, Highland's seventh administrator, discussed how in the first decade of the school teachers wanted their assistants to be considered "co-teachers": "The teaching staff was still not interested in there being a salary differential between their own salaries and that of their assistants in the classroom." This insistence for strict equality was strong, despite the fact that the teachers had college degrees, state certification, and postgraduate Montessori training.

According to Glaspy, the teachers wanted equality of pay for assistants because they wanted the assistants to take more teaching responsibility in the classroom during the time they were there. Teachers worked full-time, assistants worked half-time, and the assistants made exactly half the teachers' salary. As a result the teaching assistants were the highest paid "aides" in the entire metropolitan area, and the teachers were the lowest paid among teachers.

After 1982 teachers received higher pay in order just to retain them, but assistants continued to be much more involved than their counterparts who worked in the public Montessori magnet schools. In those schools, aides were clock-punchers who would not think of taking over the class in the teacher's absence. Roles are much more rigidly defined in the public school system.

Everyone Pitches In
Egalitarianism at Highland stands out in other ways. For example, a former parent board president decreed that it was good for children to see the board president cleaning toilets. The celebration of diversity reinforces egalitarianism, although it runs counter to prevailing cultural norms which would have us seek higher places over others.

Egalitarianism does not say that everyone is equal, however; it says that everyone is to be equally respected, and that to the extent they are able, everyone is to contribute in every way they can to the enterprise of the school. Not everyone contributes as they should, though. Some people in poverty are "client-like"—they avoid involvement, fearing failure and embarrassment or because they do not appreciate the amount of work this small school requires in order to survive. "Consumer" parents do not have or wish to spend the time on such mundane activities, especially on fund-raising or workdays.

There is an ongoing echo of, "It's hard to motivate parents; it's hard to get them involved." But this is the plaint of the perfectionist. For Highland's spirit is one of seeking perfection, not by measuring itself in some quantitative terms, but by fiercely—I use that word deliberately—holding to its values: diversity, community, respect, caring, nurturing, egalitarianism, nonviolence. "We have to succeed," that former board president told me years ago, "and we will." In athletics that attitude would be called intensity or competitiveness. At Highland it flows from a basic toughness: We *will* do whatever we must to nurture each other and rejoice in our differences because we can learn so much from each other. We *will* be gentle in a violent neighborhood.

Highland's Value of Nonviolence

At the beginning of the 1994–95 school year two incidents at the school brought home to everyone at Highland how thoroughly violence had permeated their immediate surroundings. In the first, a fourteen-year-old (not a Highland student or relative) was seen playing on the playground with a handgun tucked into his pants. Teachers Pat Farrington and Tim Souers calmly asked him to leave, and he did without further incident. A few days later while the children played outside, a man was gunned down in the parking lot across the street, hit by automatic weapon fire from a passing car. This latter incident led to the creation of the "911 Drill," said by one of the staff to be the opposite of a fire drill. "In a fire drill we all learn to move outside the building quickly," he said. "In a 911 drill, we all move inside the building quickly."

Nonviolence Confronts Fear

Nonviolence is a term chosen deliberately by those who practice it at Highland. It is a word that harks back to the civil rights campaigns of the 1950s and 1960s, a philosophy articulated by Dr. Martin Luther King, Jr., as he confronted the oppression of black people in America, first in the South, then in the cities of the North. King suffered at the hands of those who sought to stop his fight for justice; he was jailed, beaten, ridiculed, and finally assassinated. Fear was his daily companion. His constant temptation was to either fight back physically or to run away. He would do neither.

In the face of his fear, he counseled his supporters to engage in the altruism of the Good Samaritan (King, 1963), an altruism which is *universal* (not limited to tribe, race, class, or nation), *excessive* (going beyond what is necessary), and *dangerous* (willing to risk). "The ultimate measure of a man is not where he stands in moments of comfort and convenience, but where he stands at times of challenge and controversy," wrote King (p. 25).

The daily challenge of the people of Highland may not be as dramatic as the civil rights campaigns of the South, but it requires constant courage and daily commitment not to give in to the blight of violence all around, either by engaging in it or, more likely, running from it. The roots of this conviction go back to Maria Montessori herself, who sought world peace by freeing children from the tendencies of adults to oppress them through interference and intimidation. The founders of the school all came out of the civil rights and antimilitarism movements of the 1960s. The school has always attracted individuals sympathetic to those causes.

Tim Souers himself, as the senior staff member, with a history at Highland going back to 1972, embodies these ideals of respectful engagement and resistance to the insidious erosion of the urge to violent behavior, in speech as well as behavior. Some years ago Tim was shot in the chest trying to stop a street mugger from snatching an elderly woman's purse. (He admits that he was naive about the presence of a deadly weapon, however.) And in 1988 his giving of advice to a battered mother of one of his students led to retaliation by the boyfriend, who smashed the windows of his van and later the windows of his home near the school, causing Tim for safety reasons to have to relocate his family temporarily to another neighborhood farther from the school.

Nonviolence Requires Commitment

These unusual examples of nonviolent confrontation of violence are just that, however: unusual. The daily life of the school is *not* swathed in fear. The way nonviolence pervades this daily life is through the commitment of all the adults there, staff and parents and even trustees (who meet at the school monthly), to the values that King enunciated. These adults engage in altruistic behavior which is certainly "universal, excessive, and dangerous." It is universal in its sincere involvement of the diverse people of the neighborhood. It is excessive in the sense that everyone at Highland goes beyond what the outside world would discern as necessary. It is dangerous because it risks not only the possible random violence of the street but also the comfort and security of the future in a job with lower pay and fewer monetary fringe benefits than could be found in the public schools.

Daily, as educators, Highland's teachers confront the violence of the neighborhood. "We have more rough kids now," says Tim,

kids who feel more stress from the breakdown of the neighborhood. The parents whip their kids and don't let them outside. There's a lot of fear. Sometimes the teachers have to run interference for the kid with the parents. But Highland is a parent training ground. We learn to respect each other, parents especially. Many of them don't feel good about themselves; we work on that on many levels. We also let children discover good things about themselves [through the curriculum and field trips]. Parents discover good things about themselves, *too. Parents like getting hugged. But some parents must be told off, too.*

Parent education workshops and informal contacts by teachers counsel parents on methods of disciplining their children besides physical punishment. The curriculum of Highland now includes regular time spent discussing how to resolve conflicts which the children experience. For example, "class council" in the Junior Level is a weekly meeting to discuss conflicts students may have experienced that week in school, such as rough play on the playground. The "talking feather," literally a feather passed around the circle, gives its holder the floor to speak. In another regular curricular spot, Tim takes both the Junior Level students and his Extended Day students for a time each Friday afternoon called the I Care Club. They use exercises from a workbook by Schmidt and Friedman (1991) to discuss ways to resolve real and hypothetical conflict situations young people face. Typical rules include (1) finding the problem, (2) attacking it and not the person, (3) listening to each other, (4) caring about each other's feelings, and (5) taking responsibility for what we say and do. "Fouls" include hitting, name-calling, threats, bossing, making excuses, blaming, teasing, not listening, getting even, and making putdowns.

Nonviolence Is Patient

The nurturance of children implies that adults who care for them practice patience and gentleness in their discipline of the little ones, even when the children may not be used to it. Here is a typical example from the Children's House circle time.

When Tim stands up from working with two children, he is a broad-shouldered six feet, his graying hair in a pony tail. His droopy moustache supports a straight Roman nose, which in turn balances granny glasses. He rings a little bell quietly, and everyone falls silent. "Highland Community School people, it is time to put your work away," he announces in conversational loudness. As the children start to assemble, he begins to sing "We shall overcome" as softly as he can. They join in, as softly as they can. The tiniest girl, with dozens of tight pigtails, seems lost. Tim gently scoops her up and nestles her in his lap as he sits down on the floor, quietly giving instructions to those having trouble coordinating where they sit so that they can form a circle.

Now they play the listening game. Tim picks two boys to stand in the center of the circle. "Listen," he says, "jump up and down three times—not yet, listen—then stamp your foot three times, then go sit down." He repeats the instructions. The boys do what he asked and he picks two more boys, varying the instruction to "turn around two times" instead of stamping feet. One of the boys is shy and just stands there. Tim encourages him but he still seems frozen. Tim asks a girl to stand up, hold his hand, and do it with him. The boy jumps once, but they get tangled up trying to twirl. He is mightily embarrassed as the girl sits down. Tim holds out his arms and the boy runs to bury his head in Tim's shoulder, then he sits down at Tim's request. The day is saved.

Now comes the passing-of-the-bell game: each child in turn is to carry the bell carefully across the circle and put it down in front of another child, all without making a sound. Then the carrier is free to walk outside to play on this day in late May. The tiny child on Tim's lap is the first to try and tinkles the bell several times. Two older boys laugh loudly, and Tim admonishes them gently but firmly, saying, "She's trying her best." He asks them to sit back outside the circle. One resists, and Tim simply picks him up and places him there. Tears well in the child's eyes and he kicks a nearby table in a quick outburst of rage. Tim ignores him, and he quiets down.

Suddenly, though unobtrusively, Tim is on his feet heading for the adjacent bathroom with his lap child, who had not yet left, and who had wet her pants from being upset. While he is behind the door (the game is still going on), two other boys begin to talk loudly. He opens the door, calls them to sit with the previous offenders. They do. Now there are nine left in the room. Now eight. They are all trying hard to be quiet and control themselves.

After everyone else is gone except the four boys sitting outside the circle, Tim calls them to sit in a half circle in front of him, and tells the first two that their laughter caused the little one to wet her pants. To all of them he then says solemnly, "The whole school has to help each other. Here we all help each other." He just looks at each one to see if what he has said has registered. Satisfied, he asks them to pass the bell to each other. They do and leave quietly. Circle time has taken about fifteen minutes.

At first glance Tim's modeling of patience with firmness appears to be no more than any good teacher would display. The other teachers display similar patience with their charges as well. Sitting in numerous meetings and observing informal adult interactions in the halls and on the playground, I saw the same sort of respectful patience everywhere throughout the school. This respectful patience is deliberate and often discussed. It is promoted constantly under the value of "nonviolence," because the violence of the neighborhood is a virulent pathogen seeking to infect the school at every opportunity.

Thus the diamond of nonviolence at Highland shows many facets. Highland people confront their very realistic fears of working and living in the neighborhood calmly and almost offhandedly, but not foolishly. They show commitment to the kind of altruism Dr. Martin Luther King promoted by their inclusion of every human difference found in the neighborhood, by their going well beyond the minimal efforts in their work, and by their willingness to risk. They educate deliberately for nonviolent behavior. They show each other respectful patience.

In summary, the values of nurturing children, egalitarianism, and nonviolence, all resting on the need for each individual to contribute in every way possible to the enterprise, form the fabric of Highland's community. We now turn our attention to a particular manifestation of that community, the collegiality of the staff.

The Collegiality of Highland's Staff

Let us listen in on a typical weekly staff meeting to get the flavor of collegiality that enables each member to cooperate with the others in planning Highland's operations. This meeting took place after school toward the end of the school year in 1991.

The room is another large former bedroom of the mansion; a long table is in the center of the the room. Paige Prillaman, Mary Beth Pinkerton, and Brenda DeWindt are first to arrive; Grace Renteria-Shirah, the administrative assistant, chairs the meeting. Ranard Morris, parent coordinator, arrives in short order. Tim is missing, having gone to his parents' cottage in Clear Lake, Indiana, for a three-day weekend (by staff consensus). Bob Desotelle, the administrator, will be late. He had stayed to chat with me and didn't leave for a downtown errand until twenty minutes before the meeting was to start. The Children's House assistants are not present, for reasons I do not know. Everyone else seems to understand their absence, however.

Everyone is talking animatedly at once, like a party, enjoying each other's company. Three people offer me cans of soda water, which I decline. The first item on the agenda is what to do as a treat for the graduates of the Junior Level. Brenda says, "This is a wild idea. It's stupid to tell." Urged to tell—"We like wild ideas!"—she blurts out, "Let's take them to Great America." The idea is seriously discussed but dropped because nobody's stomach is up to spending a day on the rides. Someone else suggests a party at the school with piñatas. "Come on," says Ranard, "Piñatas?" He offers instead to check on pony rides at a local park. Children wander in occasionally to speak to various staff members, then leave. Bob offers to check on the availability of dancers and magicians, which he suggests could follow "picnic-type games." "Graduation is my responsibility," he says, "I'll put it together." They agree to move to the next agenda item. Everyone seems to genuinely like each other.

Grace reports briefly on the school's health and life insurance coverage for the staff. July first will begin the school's twenty-third year, but it will be the first in which the school has offered health and life insurance to its staff. Health insurance will be through an HMO with full coverage; life insurance will be $10,000 on each individual staff person. There will not be dental coverage. The money for these benefits has yet to be raised, though Bob says he has a good idea where it'll come from, without being more specific. At times during the interchange, Ranard looks at a *Time* magazine and Bob leafs through the day's mail.

The agenda's third item is that a family outside the school's boundaries, but with special ties to Tim Souers, is requesting admission for their child. Quickly, without a formal vote, they decide to recommend denial of permission to the Admissions Committee, because only six to eight openings will be available in the fall, due to the admission of so many siblings of children already enrolled. Such siblings have priority over new families' children. I note that Highland seems to have a stronger neighborhood identity now, perhaps due to its increased visibility and popularity, than when I was the administrator two decades ago.

Two more items: Pick a day for staff meetings next year. They agree unanimously on Mondays at 3:30 pm. Bob notes that such weekly meetings are important not only for business, but also for "blowing off steam." Lastly, the staff needs to socialize at the end of the year. They'll spend their annual "retreat" at Tim's farm in northern Wisconsin June first and second; they'll go out for drinks together after graduation ceremonies; they'll go to lunch together on the last day of the school year.

The meeting takes forty minutes. A disagreement over what food they'll eat at Tim's farm brings a chortle from Ranard. "I know you guys; you'll bring sprouts and broccoli!" The three Caucasians are vegetarians; no one else is; yet everyone good-naturedly promises to compromise on food they bring to the potluck.

The ways in which the adults in the school interrelate are the models for the ways the students interact among themselves. Therefore, it is paramount that staff form collegial bonds. Roland Barth (1990), a former school principal, wrote of his concern about the adversarial relationships that exist among many school personnel, which he saw as evidence of a lack of collegiality. His solution to these negative relationships is to help school people become colleagues. An atmosphere of collegiality, he concludes, reveals four characteristic behaviors. Adults in schools *talk* to each other about their practice; they *observe* each other engaged in these practices of teaching and learning; they *engage* with each other in planning and implementing curricula; they *teach* each other what they know about teaching and learning (Barth, 1990). At Highland the scope of collegiality is broadened to include all those who work with the children in the school, because Highland's small size and democratic character enables such blurring of roles.

Highland does not employ the traditional principal model (the principal is part-time, also teaching in the Children's House and Extended Day programs; the executive director sees to the noninstructional aspects of the school's operation). But Barth's comments about how the principal can promote collegiality bear summarizing. According to Barth (p. 32), the principal can promote collegiality by stating *explicit expectations* for teachers to *cooperate* with each other. He or she should also *model* collegiality; *reward* it with released time, funds, space, and recognition; and *protect* teachers who take risks from their fellow teachers' retribution.

Barth roots his discussion of the perennial problems of staff development in the theme of relationships. The traditional approach to faculty development sees the principal as promoting teacher change through the principal's role as evaluator. But historically this role of evaluator has not produced change so much as it has produced defensiveness on both sides. Barth suggests that in order to make each teacher a "deeply engrossed student," the principal must "listen in a hundred different ways" for a question or a comment such as "Here's what I want to try," to emanate from teachers, and then be ready to "supply assistance or encouragement in a hundred different ways" (Barth, 1990, p. 33).

Some teachers can neither be self-critical nor hear criticism of themselves; others can be self-critical but can't hear it said of them. Yet others can do both, which is optimal. The principal who listens and assists "in a hundred different ways" is the principal who will help teachers be both self-critical and accepting of constructive criticism by their peers, the basis of collegiality.

A few paragraphs earlier in this section I presented a vignette of a Highland *staff* meeting; included are administrators and the cook. Highland also has *faculty* meetings in which only the teachers and their assistants meet to discuss classroom business. The one I attended during the noon hour in early October, 1994, looked in many ways like the hundreds I have sat through in the schools I've taught and worked in. But there were subtle differences.

Sitting on little chairs in Tim's Children's House classroom, Tim begins the meeting promptly for the two teachers and two assistants there. Mary Ann Erdtmann will be there shortly. A third assistant is unable to attend. Tim runs down the calendar of events for the coming months. There is quite a bit on tap. In evaluating events of the past two days first, however, last evening's Parent Education Night is described as both good and disappointing. Interaction had been good but "only" about 26 parents (from 55 families!) had shown up for the voluntary gathering. "How was Cynthia Turner, the new music teacher?" asks Tim. Eniola pronounces her "great." That comment leads to a brief interchange ending in the entire staff spontaneously singing a few bars from Joen Bettmann's "Cleanup Song."

Tim announces that next week he and Maribeth will take twenty-five Children's House students to his farm for an overnight. And also that week he will take the second- and third-graders to the Crane Foundation near Wisconsin Dells, a unique setting where whooping cranes are nurtured by representatives from countries around the world as the focal point for peace education. There will be the Parent Potluck, parent conferences, including visiting the new students' homes, and White Cane Day on November fifteenth in which a blind runner will come in as a role model (yet another Highland educational "subprogram"). The October Role Model will be a woman electrician. There follows discussion of a two-day Montessori conference at MacDowell Montessori School down the street, given by the Milwaukee Public Schools and to which Highland's teachers are invited. Joen Bettmann, former Highland teacher, will run the conference.

There is calm excitement in this interchange; the teachers and their assistants are interested in what they are doing. Other items on the agenda include starting "superhelpers" (using the older students as helpers around the school, including mentoring younger students) and book orders. They then discuss children with whom they have concerns, matter-of-factly stating what the problems are and agreeing to help each other where they can. Tim and Mary Ann refer to a disagreement they have over whether writing should first be taught in print or in cursive. They josh each other gently and the meeting is suddenly over after forty minutes as the Extended Day children file into the room.

The adults in this school obviously talk to each other about their teaching practice. They observe each other and plan together. They teach each other what they know about teaching and learning. The principal promotes this collegiality not so much by stating explicit expectations for it but by modeling it and rewarding it in whatever way he can. I know of no instances at Highland where the principal has had to protect teachers who took risks in the classroom from the retributions of their colleagues. Not surprisingly the entire staff regularly socializes with each other outside school hours.

Summary

Highland's community is the result of focusing more on inclusion of different others, respecting their differences, than on promoting community as such, in the sense of everyone being "this way or that." The school demands that everyone in it contribute to the common enterprise in every way they can, while understanding that some can do more than others. The paradox of diversity-in-unity is buttressed by three central values: valuing children highly, egalitarianism, and nonviolence. The chapter elaborated examples of each in action. At its value core Highland runs counter to the mainstream culture.

Highland's staff embodies collegiality, another aspect of community in a school. They plan together, work alongside one another, teach each other, socialize together. Thus staff members teach communitarian values at least as much by their interactions as by their words.

Having discussed Highland's values, the next five chapters discuss Highland's organizational, or programmatic, variables. Chapters 4 through 6 review parent involvement research literature and describe parental participation and governance at Highland.

Chapter Four
Recent Research on Parent Involvement

Parent involvement is strongly related to student achievement.
—Bob Desotelle, Highland's eighth administrator

In the broadest sense parent involvement in schools refers to "parents' involvement in their children's education" (Schneider and Coleman, 1993). What parents do *at home* with their children regarding their school tasks is probably the most important aspect of parent involvement. What they do *with respect to the school* regarding their children's work is another key ingredient in children's school success or failure.

This chapter divides the research literature into three parts. The first section examines the effects of socioeconomic factors on parent involvement in their children's education, both at home and in school. The second reviews the effects of parent involvement, including parental attitudes toward education, on student achievement. The third part profiles the effects of a variety of school intervention programs for disadvantaged students, which employ a heavy parent involvement component. The literature indicates that parents' involvement in their children's education is directly related to their academic achievement. And although parents who are socioeconomically disadvantaged tend to participate less in their children's education, school programs to involve parents can help offset the negative effects of poverty.

Socioeconomic Factors in Parent Involvement

This section reviews studies of the effects of different socioeconomic factors on parental participation in their children's education, whether at home or in the school. These factors include social class, gender,

and racial/ethnic differences. Family structure also makes a difference in parental participation, as does whether the family is one of
"settled livers" or "hard livers," referring to the degree of order and
control the family experiences in its daily life.

Social Class Differences

Annette Lareau (1989) investigated whether social class had any effect on parent involvement. She studied two public elementary
schools, one—Prescott—in an upper-middle-class setting—the
other—Colton—in a low-income, working-class setting. All students
were white so that race would not be a confounding factor.

At Colton, the working-class school, parents saw the education
of their children as solely the teachers' responsibility. If teachers asked
parents to monitor homework closely or to carry out other education programs at home, the parents resisted. These parents, lacking
academic self-confidence, deferred to the teachers' higher (professional) status and rarely achieved rapport with the teachers. In general, although the parents knew little about the school or its expectations for them and their children, they gave evidence they liked the
teachers and they rarely made requests of the teachers. But critical
remarks about the lunch program or of school safety indicated that
many parents had strong negative feelings about their children's experience, though not yet of the academic program. Lareau characterized these parents as "settled livers," a term from Lillian Rubin's
(1976) study of working-class white families. It connotes clean orderly lives despite low incomes and lack of sophisticating life experiences. Contrast them with low-income "hard livers" whose lives were
less under control and more subject to violence and drug abuse.

In Prescott, the upper-middle-class school, Lareau encountered
quite different parent behaviors toward educators. These parents were
visible in the classroom, intervening in classroom activities, criticiz-
ing classroom practices of teachers, and working to supplement and
reinforce the classroom experience of their children. Most of these
parents saw their role as overseeing their children's education, whereas
the working-class parents basically left it to the teachers.

Lareau observed that between ten and twenty-five different
mothers came to Prescott in a typical week to help in the classroom,
promoted by the school parent volunteer program. Parents moved

freely in and out of the classroom, often interrupting teacher lessons and class activities. Though on occasion a parent might read to a small group of children, they generally focused on their own off-spring, scolding them, prodding them for information about their work, working with them on assignments, or conducting an im-promptu parent-teacher conference. In their own words, these parents wanted "to know what's going on."

Parent Gender Differences

Not all parents of the same social class interacted equally with the school. In addition to clear differences in parent-school interaction between the social classes, Lareau found that parent gender played a considerable part as well. Mothers were far more likely to interact with teachers and others at the school than were the fathers. On a scale of increasing parent involvement, working-class fathers ranked lowest, upper-middle-income mothers highest. The affluent fathers were involved, such as in bigger decisions affecting their children or coming to parents' nights. But a father's volunteering occasioned special teacher notice and praise, while a mother's was taken for granted. Yet Lareau noted that the upper-status women expressed more doubt and anxiety about challenging teacher practices than did the men, perhaps reflecting the effects of gender bias in our culture.

At both Colton and Prescott, whether a student was a high achiever or not influenced the parents' interactions with the teachers. At Colton high-achieving students tended to have parents who were more involved; this participation, however, was in the form of demands on the teacher for more discipline—pushing the child harder—or paying more personal attention to the student. The parents of low achievers, the majority at Colton, did not participate in the school themselves. At Prescott, the upper-middle-class school, this pattern almost reversed itself. The parents of low-achieving students were the most vocal in demanding a "personalized curriculum" for their children. Parents of high achievers were moderately involved.

Social class differences among parents and between working-class parents and teachers show up in their experience of work. The lack of participation by working-class parents might be encapsulated by this logic: "I work from nine to five, then I go home, leaving work behind. My child goes to school from eight to three. That's their work; they leave it behind and come home." In other words, the parents' experience of work colors their perception of their children's education and their own place in it.

The teachers at Colton resented this view because it differed so drastically from their own. A teacher, as a middle-class professional, "takes work home" in the sense that the work, being primarily mental, carries over into evenings, weekends, summers. Prescott parents shared this experience of work; they were doctors, lawyers, professors, and other professionals who "carried their work with them." According to Lareau, this class gulf in views of work underlies a large part of the separation between working-class home and middle-class school. It also reinforces teacher reluctance to involve parents in the actual classroom operation, because doing so is "messy."

Differences Between "Hard Livers" and "Settled Livers"

What about parents who are "hard livers," who don't even have the experience of working nine to five, whose experience is the debilitating poverty of the inner city? The following quotation from Alexander Mood gives us a window on their lives:

Poor families . . . are endlessly forced to trade time for money—to search for work, to moonlight, to find cheap food, to seek out an acceptable inexpensive place to live, to try to find cheap second-hand spare parts for a disabled car or appliance, to try to find out how to replace the parts themselves or to try to find a knowledgeable neighbor who can spare a little time to help them out, to search for a person who would loan a little money in an emergency at less than a confiscatory rate of interest, to struggle with the vast complication of bureaucracies . . . to stave off frightening installment collectors in order to catch up with payments to even more frightening ones, to plead with merchants who have overcharged them to be merciful, to lose one's way in the maze of public transportation trying to get a day's work in a strange neighborhood, to walk and walk and walk when one does not have busfare, to entreat the landlord to honor his commitment, to trudge all day through the mystifying maze of the county hospital with a crying sick child in search of a little reassurance, to endure sneering petty persons who dispense public service to the poor. The debilitating struggle to keep alive without money in a complex, highly organized society is so frightening, so humiliating, so emotionally exhausting, that one's patience and strength are totally spent when one finally gets home to one's children. (Webb & Sherman, 1990, p. 415)

The only element missing from this portrait of the "hard life" is the fear of violence, increasingly a staple of drug-sodden, depressed neighborhoods.

John Ogbu (1974) studied how poor black families on welfare in Stockton, California, interacted with the teachers in their children's schools. The social class gulf that Lareau found existed between working-class parents and teachers yawned even greater between these "hard livers" and teachers, exacerbated by deeper poverty and racial attitudes which widened the gap further. Stockton parents all too frequently adapted to this gulf in a variety of self-defeating ways, often blaming themselves for problems in communication and their children's failures in school or seeing themselves as "victims of a bad neighborhood." When they did shift blame to the school, however, Ogbu found that they could not explain how the school was miseducating their children other than by vague references to racism. But instead of stepping up their contacts with school personnel, too many withdrew in sullen anger and fear, thinking they could not change anything at the school.

In Lareau's study the teachers at both schools did not seem to behave differently regarding the social class differences of the students and parents. Parent involvement to these teachers was traditional. They wanted all parents to adhere to the four Rs: Read to your children, Reinforce the curriculum, Respond to teacher requests, Respect the teacher's professionalism. Parents, they felt, should prepare their children for school, including reading to them and teaching them number concepts, as well as nurturing them and interacting with them. Parents should attend school events, such as parent-teacher conferences; they should fulfill requests teachers make of them, such as playing word games with their children or providing a second pair of pants for school in case the child should soil the first. They should monitor homework, if there is any. All teachers would support these parental involvement requirements.

At both schools, however, parents were on their own to become further involved. Accordingly, social class differences, with the huge discrepancies in income and education and corresponding effects on how persons see their ability to intervene on their children's behalf, affected how and whether parents intervened. Things were worse in Ogbu's study: teachers saw themselves as missionaries to a backward people and often became the "petty persons who dispense public service to the poor" mentioned earlier. Lareau and Ogbu both concluded that schools would have to adapt to parents, especially to the working-class poor.

Family Structure Differences

Schneider and Coleman (1993), in a massive study of 26,000 eighth-graders and their families, discovered that families with "traditional structure" (i.e., two parents in the home as opposed, for example, to single parents, separated or divorced parents, and so forth) scored higher on several measures of parent involvement. They were more likely to know the parents of their children's friends at school. They were more likely to discuss daily school matters with their children at home. Their children were likelier as students to have a sense of psychological well-being.

Racial/Ethnic Differences

Schneider and Coleman (1993) also traced differences among ethnic/racial groups with regard to parental involvement in school. Asian American parents tended not to know the parents of their children's friends and were least likely to be involved in school activities, but they scored highest in restricting their children's TV watching, in enrolling their children in extra classes, and in saving for college. They spent generously on their children's education. African Americans were most likely to help their children in planning their high school program and to participate in the parent teacher organization (PTO). They were also the most likely to contact the school about matters concerning their children. Hispanics spent more on educational expenses for their children than any other group and were more likely to restrict their children's TV viewing than either whites or African Americans. White parents had the highest parental involvement in school when it included a social component, such as attending school functions.

Summary of Socioeconomic Factor Effects on Parent Involvement

Socioeconomic factors do influence whether parents become involved in their children's education. Without special school programs to promote parent involvement, middle-class parents will be more likely to contact the school and make demands on behalf of their children than will working-class parents. Women will be more likely to take the initiative to be involved than will men. "Hard living" parents are more likely to engage in self-defeating behaviors with regard to their children's schooling. Parents from traditional (two-parent) families will be more likely to be involved in the home with their children's school affairs than will parents from nontraditional families.

Racial or ethnic differences, holding social class factors constant, will influence parental involvement. Asian Americans may be less likely to contact the school, but are more likely to set high standards for their children's education and monitor them. African Americans are most likely to be involved in school matters on their children's behalf. Hispanics also are more likely to be involved in their schools than are whites.

The Effects of Parent Involvement on Student Achievement

Studies of the effects of parental influence at home on children's academic success agree that socioeconomic factors and whether the mother works outside the home can affect the parents' ability to *act* on their educational expectations for their children (e.g., Schneider and Coleman, 1993; Snow et al., 1991; Klimes-Dougan et al., 1992; Clark, 1983). But parental attitude toward their children's schoolwork can be a deciding factor in whether the children achieve or not.

A Study of Parental Attitudes toward School Achievement

Reginald Clark (1983) studied ten families in Chicago, five of which had high achievers in high school and five low achievers. All were black and all were very poor. Clark studied the interactions between the parents and children in these families which influenced the children's success or failure in school. Of the five families which had successful students, two had both parents in the home, three had single parents. The low-achieving families had a similar structural configuration.

The parents of the high-achieving students, despite the shackles placed on them by lack of money and resources, had several similar strategies: (1) They encouraged literacy in their children by reading to them, by encouraging them to read and write about topical issues, and by talking to them about what they read and wrote. (2) They practiced social etiquette, engaged in word games, and encouraged hobbies. (3) Although parents gave instructions, they allowed feedback; they "communicated interactively," in Clark's term. (4) Discipline was firm but not harsh, and the emotional climate was supportive.

Clark discovered that the poverty-level parents of high achievers "sponsored their independence." They defined the limits of appropriate behavior (a duty far too many middle-class parents shirk), allocated money and other resources to the extent they could, and delegated responsibility to these adolescents. The young people in turn gained multiple opportunities for initiative in structuring their homework tasks, leisure tasks, and household maintenance tasks. Parents set schedules and routines, monitored their children's friends and other social contacts, and taught them self-protection.

The family life of the low-achieving students Clark studied fit the stereotypes of parent styles of poverty-level families commonly described (Webb & Sherman, 1990): authoritarian, punishment-oriented, with only sporadic warmth or affection. Parental interest was only in the consequences of children's behavior, not in why it was done. These parents had internalized and conveyed to their offspring that their behaviors made no difference and that they were to be judged more by others than by themselves. Forget the painful past, their actions taught. Focus on the present and assume no future, because the world is harsh and cruel. Develop physical toughness, conformity, acceptance, docility. These parents could not succeed as parents because they themselves had been too crushed as children.

Clark demonstrated, however, that there are parents who succeed incredibly well in spite of damning circumstances. Though he did not study the effects of school policy on how well these parents were able to interact with their youngsters, other studies have done so.

Effects of Parental Involvement on Literacy Achievement

Catherine Snow and her associates (1991) tested the effects of three models of parental involvement on four outcomes of low-income children's development of literacy skills: word recognition, vocabulary, writing production, and reading comprehension. The first two models, which they called "The Family as Educator Model" and "The Resilient Family Model," focused only on measures within families, such as quality of parent-child interaction, whether parents involved children in learning activities outside school such as music lessons or computer camps, whether the mother was active in neighborhood betterment efforts, and degree of organization or stress in the family. These two models explained (correlated with) some of the children's literacy improvement, which comprised two or three of the four outcome variables.

But a third model, "The Family in Partnership with School Model," was the most powerful of the three, showing significant correlations with all four outcome measures. That is, where teachers initiated contact with parents on a regular basis about academic (not disciplinary) matters regarding their children, the children showed gains in academic achievement over controls, including over two years' worth in reading comprehension. Several other studies cited by Snow indicated that school-initiated contacts with families increased teachers' and parents' ratings of each other, reduced truancy and behavior problems, and increased the parents' understanding of what their children were being taught.

In a follow-up study described in the same text, Snow and her associates confirmed that the family's "provision of literacy" was the most powerful predictor of children's literacy success four years later. Other important factors were maternal education and maternal expectations for the child's education. Measures of parental involvement in the home were as follows:

- The parents talked to the children at home about school matters and their educational futures without nagging.
- Parents involved their children in educational activities outside school, for example, music lessons, computer camp.
- Parents implemented rules regarding TV-watching and homework, for example, they provided adequate space and help when needed.
- Parents knew the parents of the schoolmates of their children.
- Parents saw that their children attended school and got there on time.
- Parents "provided literacy" for their children by reading to them books and giving them books.
- The mother was active outside the home.

Snow and her associates demonstrated that in-home parent involvement was essential to children's academic achievement and that it could be facilitated by excellent school conditions and policies promoting parent involvement.

Further Research on Parent Involvement and Student Achievement

Schneider and Coleman (1993) studied the families of eighth-graders to determine the relationship between parental values—and the actions they take in the home as a result—and student achievement, including social development. Their outcome measures were standardized test scores, grades, and reports of student misbehavior.

Four factors influenced the extent to which parents participated in the education of their children: motivation, financial and other resources, time constraints, and school policies which hindered or encouraged parent involvement. Parental time constraints and school policies were more important factors than expected. Mothers working full-time had much less time for after-school supervision than did mothers working part-time or not at all. And after-school supervision was the in-home factor most highly related to test scores and grades. (The others were talking about current school experiences with the children, frequent parental TV restriction, child enrolled in outside class such as music, and the number of parents of child's friends known.)

Study of school policy focused on what schools did to promote greater teacher-parent contact. The characteristics of the school staff, that is, their racial/ethnic composition and their efforts to reach out to the parents, were the chief determiners of school-parent communication. Guidance of students to the next level (i.e., high school) and formal pressures on students to progress academically were not related to teacher-parent communication. In schools with large minority populations, it was not surprising to find that parents felt most comfortable interacting with teachers of their own race or ethnicity.

Summary of Parent Involvement Effects on Student Achievement

In-home parental involvement most influences children's academic achievement. Even in the midst of the direst poverty, some parents are able to successfully interact with their children and help them succeed academically. They "provide literacy": they read to their children and let them read to them in turn, they encourage their children's writing, and they talk to their children about what the children read and write. They practice social etiquette, show them how to protect themselves, and encourage hobbies. Their discipline is firm, but not harsh. And above all, they *listen* to their children as well as give them rules.

Successful parents "sponsor their children's independence." They set limits on their behavior, including TV viewing hours and required times for homework, and they monitor them. They give their children resources to the extent they can, and they monitor their friendships. They find educational activities for their children outside school, such as field trips or camps, and the mother is active outside her home, one place for her activism being the school.

If schools can adapt to the life conditions of their parents and children, they will promote parental involvement in their own children's education. The next section reviews research on educational programs that involved disadvantaged parents as a means to boost their children's academic achievement.

The Effects of School Intervention Programs
that Promote Parent Involvement

This section is an overview of early childhood and early elementary programs for disadvantaged children, including Head Start, which have relied to varying degrees on parent participation. A separate succeeding section reviews the James Comer "process" for involving parents in their children's elementary schools.

Early Childhood Programs for Disadvantaged Children

Robert E. Slavin and his associates (1994a) reviewed several hundred studies of a wide variety of programs designed to improve the reading skills of disadvantaged students. The early intervention programs studied were of three types: (1) those intervening *before* formal reading instruction begins, including preschool, kindergarten, and even infancy development programs; (2) programs affording *additional time* before full-scale reading instruction begins, such as retention in kindergarten or first grade, or a "transitional first grade" (an extra year); and (3) interventions in *first grade and beyond*. The earliest intervention programs (1) were also categorized as "high, moderate, and low intensity." "High intensity" meant long duration, extended daily time, low teacher-child ratio, and considerable staff-parent interaction. "Moderate intensity" and "low intensity" were accordingly less on these variables.

Intervention Before Formal Reading Instruction Begins

High-intensity programs, such as the Milwaukee Project and the University of North Carolina's Abecedarian Project, showed impressive gains in children's IQs, language proficiency skills, and other measures from infancy to three, but where there was no follow-up, they were not maintained over time. Some of these programs focused primarily on intervention with parents, others with children, still others equally with each.

Moderate-intensity programs focusing solely on working with parents, such as the Gordon Parent Education Project, showed mixed results. In the case of the Gordon Project, for example, intervention for two to three years led to greater gains than for one year only, which showed no gain at all. Low-intensity programs, such as the Verbal Interaction Project's Mother-Child Home Program, in which paraprofessionals demonstrated educational toys every week or two in the home for two to three years, showed either no effects or no long-term effects.

Slavin and his associates concluded from these "earliest intervention" program studies that the more intense the intervention with the parent and with the child the better; that focus on parent education alone is insufficient—the child must be included in the intervention; that center-based programs, rather than home-based, were more successful; and that the longer the intervention (and follow-up) the better. The degree of intensity (the higher the better) was the most important factor overall.

The BEEP Program for Infants, Toddlers, and Prekindergartners

Many of the above conclusions are corroborated in a unique experiment in Brookline, Massachusetts—the Brookline Early Education Project, or BEEP (Hauser-Cram et al., 1991). Using foundation grants to support educational and health components, the developers of BEEP employed the public elementary schools of Brookline as centers for an intensive infants, toddlers, and prekindergarten program to prepare children for entry into kindergarten. BEEP offered three levels of program intensity—low, moderate, and high—to the families of Brookline, using pediatricians to disseminate information.

The BEEP program included all categories of children; its first group of 282 children included 37 percent who were minorities and 17 percent whose first language was other than English. The moderate- and high-intensity levels included respite child care, and home visits, but all children received extensive diagnostic and physical exams, and their parents participated in parent discussion groups. All toddlers (1–3 years) participated in weekly playgroups and all prekindergartners (3–4 years) participated in daily prekindergarten programming with optional extended day care.

To evaluate BEEP, whose ultimate purpose was to reduce school failure, researchers measured classroom competence on an eight-attribute scale using classroom observation and teacher ratings. Results showed that BEEP children were significantly less likely than comparison children to exhibit problems in kindergarten or the second grade. BEEP was particularly effective with children whose mothers had less education but were participants in the high intensity programming. Again, a high-intensity, center-based, long-term program that works with both parents and children is most likely to produce later school success.

One particularly interesting finding in the BEEP research was that many parents did not find the structured discussions about parenting issues very useful. Some low-income parents were not accustomed to such an open format, were inhibited by one or two parents who dominated the discussion, or felt that their problems were not understood in context (e.g., the problems a single parent faces in a low-income housing project are different from those a single parent faces in a middle-class neighborhood).

Other Preschool Programs

Slavin and his associates (1994) next investigated whether preschool programs alone could prevent early school failure. David Weikart's well-known Perry Preschool Project, a twenty-year longitudinal study which has been cited as evidence of the need to extend Head Start to a wider clientele, unfortunately did not contain academic achievement measures that fit the Slavin format (Weikart's program was not a Head Start program, however). Martin Deutsch's intervention, which was the forerunner of the Head Start Program, showed that the magnitude of cognitive effects was relatively small even with continued intervention. The Perry Project had a low-intensity parent component; Deutsch's had none.

Head Start Thirty Years On

Project Head Start is relevant to our discussion because of its national scope, its political popularity, and its heavy emphasis on involving parents in their children's educational development. One former parent of Highland likened the school to a Head Start program, although there are significant differences, the principal one being that Head Start is a one-year program for four-year-olds whereas Highland is a six-year program for ages 3 to 9. Highland doesn't have a comprehensive health program, as does Head Start.

Under President Lyndon Johnson, Head Start was launched in 1965 as a summer program for 100,000 disadvantaged four-year-old children across the United States. Despite many setbacks and crises, by 1993 Head Start was serving about 700,000 poor children, or about 3 of every 10 eligible, in year-long programs (although only 15 percent of these are full-*day* programs). It was the first publicly funded comprehensive developmental program for young children that incorporated parents as full participants. Head Start's approach is comprehensive because it includes health, nutrition, and social service components as well as classroom educational activities (which follow a variety of curricular models).

Hiring and training parents of Head Start children is also a high priority; by 1987 about a third of Head Start staff nationwide were parents of current or former students (Washington & Oyemade, 1987). Its $7 billion annual budget continues to be administered by the Department of Health and Human Services rather than by the Department of Education. Its cost per child in 1990, however, was $2,803, about equal to what Highland spends. In other words, it continues to be seriously underfunded.

The Role of Parents in Head Start. Bessie Draper, Head Start's first Parent Program Specialist in 1966, wanted low-income parents to be full partners in their own children's development (Zigler & Meunchow, 1992). To accomplish this goal of "maximum feasible parent participation," Head Start's parent involvement policy listed four major functions for parents. Parents should (1) participate in decision making about the nature and operation of their programs; (2) participate in the classroom as paid employees, volunteers, and observers; (3) receive home visits from Head Start staff; and (4) participate in educational activities. But the parent role stopped short of exclusive control by parents. The overall goal of the policy was to balance the empowerment of parents as decision makers and the use of parent involvement as a tool to educate them.

Head Start's Motivating Effects. How has Head Start's emphasis on parent involvement affected children's learning? There has been strong anecdotal evidence through the years that involving parents has helped improve their skills in promoting their children's education. Edward Zigler, Director of the Office of Child Development (Head Start's umbrella agency) for a number of years and professor of psychology at Yale University, offered this anecdote as an example:

"What difference has Head Start made to your family?" I remember asking a Head Start mother who approached me some years ago after a speech. "Well, it's simple," she said. "When my daughter used to give me pictures she had drawn, I'd think to myself, that's the ugliest picture I've seen, and wad it up and toss it in the wastebasket. After she was in Head Start, I'd take the picture, ask her to tell me about it, and post it proudly on the bulletin board." (Zigler & Meunchow, 1992, p. 114)

Head Start sought to "entice" parents more deeply into participating in their children's lives, rather than requiring it. When Harold Hines's son returned home from his Head Start center in Miami one day in 1966 with a different set of clothes on than he'd worn that morning, Harold asked him why. The child said he'd messed his pants and that the teacher had bathed him and washed his clothes. "At the time," said Harold, "I would've beaten the hell out of my son for such behavior." Hearing the teacher had meted out no punishment, Harold was impressed. "I thought about somebody showing that kind of love to my child, and the next morning I went to the school to meet the teacher. She handed me my son's clothes from the previous day, all washed and ready to wear the next day." Moved by this kindness and determined not to let the teacher's love overshadow his own, Hines began attending center meetings, became president of the council, and ultimately was hired as the parent involvement coordinator for the entire Head Start program serving Dade County (Zigler & Meunchow, 1992, p. 105).

The first major study of Head Start, the "Ohio/Westinghouse" report (Cicirelli, 1969) was highly critical of the program (and highly criticized as well), but acknowledged that more than 80 percent of Head Start parents thought their children had improved as a result of the program. Since poor parents have a tendency to lose hope for their children, authorities thought that any program that could raise their aspirations would help to shape their children's accomplishments. As Zigler has long held, perhaps the most important effect of Head Start or any program that intervenes to offset the disadvantages of poverty is motivating children to learn. The debate over whether programs can raise IQ or not hasn't been resolved—Zigler doesn't believe they can (Zigler & Meunchow, 1992, p. 14)—but given the right environment, they can enhance motivation to improve. The right environment obviously includes parents as a significant part.

Assessment of Head Start's Effects on Student Achievement. Formal assessments of Head Start children's achievement have varied in quality, just as the centers themselves have varied considerably. Valora Washington and Ura Jean Oyemade (1987) reviewed studies of Head Start over the first two decades of the program. Studies in the first ten years tended to agree that achievement gains faded out after three years or sooner, or as one study put it, the Head Start children reach a plateau and the control children catch up. Most of these studies were criticized for their lack of randomness, their use of controls who were not as disadvantaged as Head Start children, their narrow focus on IQ, and their assumption that one approach works for all children.

Later evaluations, including a synthesis of 210 previous research projects done on Head Start, showed a variety of positive outcomes. Although IQ or achievement score gains continued to fade out, in some studies Head Start children showed evidence of school success: fewer absences, fewer retentions in grade, and fewer assignments to special education. And there were *immediate* positive effects on children's cognitive ability, after all. There were also *immediate* socioemotional gains as well: self-esteem, social behavior, achievement motivation. Children's health improved, because Head Start generated parents' increased use of educational, health, and social services on behalf of their children.

In summary, Head Start is effective despite several handicaps. I have mentioned underfunding, which leads to teacher turnover and health and social services stretched too far. Head Start legislation does not allow for purchase of permanent facilities, only rental or upgrading of buildings, forcing many centers into an unsettling peripatetic existence. Zigler and Meunchow (1992, pp. 211–240) recommend: (a) extending Head Start into infants and toddlers programs, (b) partnering with the Chapter I program to extend Head Start into elementary school, and (c) raising the income eligibility guidelines to allow in the millions of children who could benefit, but whose parents make a little more than poverty-level wages.

Intervention in First Grade and Beyond

Looking at other strategies to educate disadvantaged students, Slavin and his associates (1994a) concluded that piecemeal approaches were useless. Their studies of full-day versus half-day kindergarten, one-year versus two-year kindergarten, and variations in entering age for kindergarten showed no differences in student achievement. Retention of children for a grade, the creation of "developmental kindergartens," and the insertion into the school of "transitional first grade" programs also showed no effects.

Reducing class size *substantially* (25 to 20 is not "substantial"; 25 to 15 is) did significantly improve achievement in grades one through three, but not for grades four and beyond. Reducing class size in first grade had a positive effect on achievement, but it faded. Slavin therefore recommended reducing class size substantially in first grade for disadvantaged students. Classroom aides, if they implement structured one-to-one tutoring programs, rather than function as "strolling troubleshooters, custodians, or clerics," can help improve disadvantaged students' achievement substantially. In general, ability grouping doesn't work.

"Success For All"

Slavin and his associates (1994b) describe a comprehensive approach to prevention of school failure through early intervention, called "Success For All," which has been replicated in many schools nationally. Its components include: excellent preschool and kindergarten programs; the improvement of curriculum, instruction, and class management throughout the grades; frequent assessment of student progress; the establishment of cooperative relationships with parents so they can support their child's learning at home; one-to-one tutoring of first-graders with reading problems by certified teachers; and relentlessly persevering with each child until that child is succeeding.

Success For All programs include a "family support team" in low-resource schools, consisting of the Parent Liaison, the Vice-Principal (if any), Counselor (if any), a facilitator, and appropriate staff already present in the school. This team provides truancy follow-up, parent education if parents desire it, and assistance for problems the family may be facing. Success For All showed only 15.7 percent of its students at least one year below grade level in third grade, compared with 38 percent of control group students. At all costs, Slavin warns, avoid retention and special education. His message, boiled down, is prevention of cumulative deficits by means of early intervention, *relentless, continuing* intervention.

Although parent cooperation with school personnel is important, it is not the centerpiece of Slavin's model. James Comer moves it to the heart of the educational process.

James Comer's Parent Involvement Model

James Comer, professor of psychiatry and director of Yale University's Child Study Center, emphasizes the building of relationships within a school in order to create a climate of support for children's learning. He begins his assessment of the problems of inner-city schools with an analysis of the mistrustful attitudes many of the adult actors carry toward one another. Much of my analysis of Highland is indebted to Dr. Comer's insights.

The Need to Improve Children's "Adult Surround"

In its October 2, 1989, issue, *Newsweek* magazine named Dr. Comer "Educational Innovator of the Year." Comer began his rise to national prominence after his book, *School Power*, was published in 1980. In it he analyzed how he and his colleagues had intervened to help improve two inner-city New Haven public elementary schools. His goals were simple but extraordinarily difficult to achieve: make each school a place for learning by improving the relationships among all the adults.

His was to be an answer to Bruno Bettelheim's concern that the nurturers of children might not be nurtured themselves. Comer sought to insure that those who care for children—both teachers and parents—would be cared for by their comrades in return. In 1968, when he began, parents had grown suspicious of school personnel, teachers had felt powerless, administrators had become frustrated. The adults were burdened with anger and depression about their present experience with the schools.

Comer reasoned that only as the adults in the school began to cooperate harmoniously would the children take notice, feel good about being in school, and learn what adults had to teach. Half a century ago a child grew up under the formal and informal tutelage of adults who knew each other. Most children had an "adult surround" that was consistent and supportive. Parents, the pastor, the principal, teachers, neighbors, and others important in the child's life all were acquainted with one another, respected each other, and to a large extent agreed on what was important to learn.

Under the impetus of technological change, however, everyone's world has become more complex, and the "distances" between adults significant in a child's life have grown longer and longer, to the point in all too many cases where consistency has been lost altogether. A child now receives information from many sources, principally television, electronic music, and slick targeted magazines that offer values conflicting with tradition, emphasizing consumption and questioning adult authority. Parental time with families has dwindled seriously under the pressure of both parents having to work. Although today's young people are no more mature for their age than their counterparts of half a century ago, Comer argues, they are by default required to make more decisions on their own about what is and is not important in their lives. The result is severely increased stress and much more dysfunctional behavior in more young people, which in turn burdens society at large with ever-increasing social costs. Comer's antidote is to involve parents and other adults more consciously in the lives of children and adolescents. His concrete way of doing so is a model of parent participation in their children's school life.

The Program Model
The model that evolved from Comer's early experience in New Haven and which is now being implemented in more than fifty schools around the country contains four components (Comer, 1985; Comer, 1988c):

The Mental Health Team
In his original project, Comer and his mental health colleagues from Yale's Child Study Center spent long hours helping build the partnerships among teachers, administrators, and parents necessary for the harmonious adult surround he advocates. Studies of his model implemented in other schools admit that the regular presence of an

individual or individuals who can help people get over the barriers between them is essential to his change agenda.

The mental health team in a typical "Comer School" would consist of at least one mental health professional (a counselor, social worker, or other professional skilled in helping people engage in dialogue with one another), a teacher, a parent, and an administrator. This team would work with all other components in the school: teachers, administration, parents, others in the community, and students.

The mental health team would work in several ways within the school environment. The team would help staff identify children who need special services and may consult on setting up individualized programs for these children. It may facilitate interactions between teachers and parents and provide training workshops and consultations to staff and parents on child development and human relations issues. The team would work particularly closely with the School Governance and Management Body, the second major component of Comer's model.

The School Governance and Management Body
This group would include the principal, a mental health team member skilled in facilitation, and representatives selected by teachers and parents. Meeting on a regular basis, the Governance Team would plan the school schedule and curriculum, allocate resources, and establish policy guidelines in all aspects of the school program. Given that these teams would exist within urban public school systems, their degrees of autonomy with respect to the central office would vary. Comer insists, however, that this Governance Team be powerful enough to make and implement policy throughout the school. Discussion of local school councils and site-based management strategies follows in chapter 6.

The Parents Program
Central to parent involvement in Comer's original project was the presence in each classroom of one parent as classroom assistant for ten hours a week. With this core group of parents as involved leaders, all parents were thus encouraged to become members of the parent-teacher group and to help run and participate in special pro-

grams at the school for families. Comer speaks of three levels of parent involvement (1988c): (a) shaping policy through their representatives on the Governance Team, (b) participating in activities supporting the school program, and (c) attending school events.

In the original intervention in New Haven, Comer and his associates had a school social worker devote time to helping parents work in the school, first as volunteers and later as classroom aides assisting teachers in academic and social aspects of the curriculum. About a dozen parents became aides; they also became the core of the parent group, planning events and activities to support the school's goals. Comer states simply and forcefully the effects of involving parents:

When we ask low-income, minority-group children to achieve in school— an instrument of mainstream society—we are often asking them to be different from their parents. With parents involved there is no conflict. (1988b, p. 29)

The Curriculum and Staff Development Program

In his New Haven Project, Comer focused on the specific needs of teachers. His program sought to integrate the various elements of the curriculum into a coherent whole, in order to foster social skills development among both students and teachers. In other words, the content of the curriculum was to be used to build relationships among all the participants in the school. The curriculum units which parents and Mental Health Team members saw were needed for low-income student populations were units in government and politics, business and economics, health and nutrition, and leisure and spiritual activities. After teachers took workshops in these new content areas, they also participated in workshops geared to improve relations among adults (staff and parents), between adults and children, and among students themselves. Each workshop showed how the new curriculum material could be used to build these relationships.

Putting oneself in the shoes of another was a giant step toward achieving positive solutions for many problems plaguing these schools. For example, when five-year-olds couldn't sit still for the hour of assembly, teachers came to understand that these students should make their presentation first, then leave at an early hour and not disrupt everyone else. As another example, the social worker, psychologist, and special education teacher worked as a team instead of separately. Teachers and parents learned through workshops run by the Yale Child Study Center staff how to respond to misbehavior with insight instead of knee-jerk retaliation. When they imagined themselves in the shoes of these youngsters and how they felt, it became easier for them to move away from reliance on punishment as their principal means of social control and toward alternative ways to help these youngsters control themselves. Comer cited the benefits of focusing on helping children control themselves in conflict situations:

When relationships improve in the schools, the children themselves become the carriers of desirable values. At the beginning of the fourth year [of the Project], someone stepped on the foot of a transfer student and his dukes went up. Another youngster said, "Hey man, we don't do that in this school." He looked at the expressions on the faces around him and read, "We don't fight," and he dropped his fists. (Comer, 1988b, p. 31)

"We knew when to fight and when not to fight," Comer writes of his own family experience.

We knew how to protect our rights in ways other than fighting. But again, we weren't born wise in skills. We were carefully taught and strongly encouraged to develop the needed skills and personal controls. We had many opportunities to use them at home, at church, and among friends before our skills were tested and judged in school. When we failed we were given sympathy and encouragement to try again. (Comer, 1988a, pp. 220–21)

Schools, he thought, could teach students who have not had this background from home to present themselves as well-behaved, bright, and able. Manners and socially acceptable problem-solving behaviors are integrated into all the new areas of the curriculum in a Comer process school.

Here is a fuller example of how the social skills curriculum worked for both children and adults: A mayoral election was impending as the politics and government unit was being developed.

Children wrote letters to the candidates, inviting them to speak to the classes, then wrote thank-you notes after they spoke. Students learned how to be hosts for parents, candidates, and staff. They learned to raise pointed but polite questions for the candidates; they also put on a dance-drama program, along with the presentations by the candidates, for the parents. Comer noted that many of the parents, witnessing all this participation by their children, actually voted for the first time in their lives.

Results of Comer's Model Implemented in Public Schools

The Original Two New Haven Elementary Schools

The Iowa Test of Basic Skills in reading and mathematics was given yearly from 1969 to 1984 to fourth-graders at the Martin Luther King, Jr., and Katharine Brennan Elementary schools. The mean scores rose gradually from well below grade level norms to about a grade above the norm in 1979, when they leveled off (Comer, 1985).

Ten Mainly Black Elementary Schools in Prince Georges County, Maryland

Among ten schools in Prince Georges County, the average percentile gains on California Achievement Test scores for third- and fifth-graders in math, reading, and language were larger for the ten schools that used Comer's model than for the district as a whole. Although the test scores of black students lagged behind those of white students, the gap narrowed in those schools that used Comer's model. Sixty-two percent of the district's 105,000 students were black, but the populations of the ten Comer process schools were closer to 90 percent black. These ten schools received extra funds because they were "hard to integrate" (Comer, 1988c).

Shepherd Zeldin (1991) studied the implementation of the Comer Process in one of these Prince Georges County schools, Barnaby Manor Elementary in Oxon Hill. In 1985 leaders of Barnaby Manor, a school with low morale and high rates of teacher and student turnover, invited Dr. Comer to help them make radical changes. Comer established two formal groups at Barnaby Manor to enable the collaboration among adults to grow. In each the explicit rules were few but strict: no blame, consensus where possible, open expression of feelings and issues.

The main decision-making group at Barnaby Manor was the School Planning and Management Team (SPMT), composed of the principal and elected teacher, parent, and staff representatives. Its job was to create a comprehensive school plan and a calendar of events for the year. The second formal decision-making group created at this school was titled the Student Staff Services Team (SSST) and was composed entirely of staff: principal, guidance counselor, teachers, psychologist, health aide, special educators, and other appropriate personnel. Meeting often, its purpose was to avoid fragmentation of services to children and to promote coherence of curriculum. This team may be thought of as the mental health team with elements of curriculum planning added to its agenda.

Although Zeldin's study did not discuss in detail how these teams were formed and whether Comer or some other "mental health intervener" facilitated the open expression of feelings and issues, it did mention problems in implementing the model. For example, the faculty members who didn't endorse the Comer process went elsewhere over time. But the "weeding out" process took six years. The faculty who remained gave the process high marks, because as one of them said, "every teacher knows what I'm doing with the students, and I know what's happening in other classes. We have the same goals, we all operate under the same rules and standards."

A second difficulty was the heavy reliance on the charisma of the principal. Zeldin voiced concern whether the "Comer process" would continue if this strong central figure left. A third difficulty was that several staff thought the central district exerted too much pressure to test students using standardized testing, thereby shaping the curriculum too much to fit these tests. Funding cuts had eaten into staff energies by spreading staff thinner. Nonetheless, maintaining good relationships between teachers, parents, and students remained the pivotal goal of the Comer process at Barnaby Manor.

Summary of the Comer Model

James Comer's model is geared toward rebuilding relationships that have broken down within schools. Where it does so, through the use of representative teams to plan and implement policy throughout the school, the theory of the positive effect of establishing an adult surround to support children's learning seems verified. Anecdotal reports, test score information, and improved attendance records suggest that Comer is correct in his idea about the importance of the adult surround. But as every study indicates, the creation of trusting teamwork is a never-ending process, sometimes taking two steps back for every step forward. Face-to-face decision making, however, about real issues, where there is real power and real responsibility, is the only route to overcoming what Comer called the "sociocultural misalignment" between home and school in poor urban districts.

Where Robert Slavin focused primarily on changing school programming, Comer suggested there is a prior step: involving the parents in the school process itself, beginning with the classroom. Comer's central message is that most if not all educational problems are "relationship problems."

Summary of School Intervention Effects on Parental Involvement

A review of multiple studies of early childhood education programs revealed that the most effective programs (in terms of reducing at risk children's chances of later school failure) had the following characteristics:

1. They were long-term, often lasting three to five years.
2. They worked intensively with both parents and children.
3. They were center-based, rather than home-based, although home visits were an essential component.
4. They incorporated age-appropriate health and nutrition components in addition to educational programming.

Even studies which focused primarily on effective educational programming for disadvantaged students at the elementary level acknowledged the need to form alliances with parents in order to reinforce the school programs' objectives. James Comer's model, which seeks to build harmonious relationships among all adults in a school, has been effective in raising inner-city children's achievement scores in several dozen schools across the country. Comer's model takes the Head Start idea of involving the parents as paid staff as well as volunteers beyond the preschool into the elementary school. The

next two chapters describe Highland Community School's approach
to parent involvement.

Chapter Five
How Highland Involves
Its Parents

We get to the children through the parents.

Tim Souers
Highland teacher

The previous chapter reviewed studies of parent involvement in their children's education, demonstrating three outcomes. First, what parents do with their children at home regarding their education is particularly important in student achievement. Second, negative socioeconomic factors can diminish parental attitude and practice, but school programs to involve disadvantaged parents have been effective in helping them improve the ways they interact with their children at home over educational matters. Third, these programs were more effective if they were long-term, intensive, and gave meaningful roles to parents in the school.

This chapter begins to flesh out how Highland sees its parents and what roles it provides for them to be involved. Highland leaders have long been aware of differences in parental attitude toward involvement in their children's education. We first look at those attitude differences and then at the opportunities Highland provides for changing them, both directly through formal workshops and indirectly through work in the school. The chapter closes with a study of how Highland's involvement practices affect parents' interaction with their children at home.

Three Types of Parental Attitudes about School Involvement

Parental attitudes toward their own involvement in their children's school vary considerably. Highland's long experience in building a parent-centered community provides rich data on these attitudes. This section outlines three distinct (although certainly not dichotomous) patterns of outlook parents at Highland have revealed since its beginnings. I'll begin with my own experience in helping launch the school.

The Activist Attitude

Many young middle-class people moving into parenthood during the idealistic late 1960s and early 1970s wanted more say over their lives. They sought meaningful work, especially work that contributed more directly to the social good. They wanted more control over their own consumption, forming cooperatives to buy healthier food and less ecologically destructive products. Sometimes they altered older religious rites to fit their worldview. They started schools for their toddlers.

The young people who started Highland were a mixture of those whose children would immediately benefit from it, those whose children would attend in a year or two, and those who had no children but cared about children anyway. We shared a deep conviction that public schools, especially those in the inner city, were dysfunctional, but felt as well that as individuals we could do little to change them. So, driven to be involved in those institutions that affected us, we took on the task of creating our own school.

We founders were activists. Though we had little money, we shared an optimism born of middle-class upbringing and education. It was the sense that, with good will, energy, and effort, we could create a new culture, at least around ourselves. We weren't self-consciously aware that we were so inclined; that realization only comes with age and reflection. But we knew something drastic had to be done, and some of us were prepared to sacrifice considerably, often postponing career and income to do it.

The Consumer Attitude

As my own two children grew up after I had left Highland in 1974, however, I came to realize begrudgingly that today's nuclear family couldn't meet all the needs of its children by itself. I couldn't keep starting schools every time my children outgrew the old ones. I began to be a school "consumer," looking for the best deal: a place with a competent staff whose values I could live with that would help my children grow emotionally and intellectually. Too often these schools were private and charged big chunks of our income for tuition. In middle and high school our two attended a small public alternative school for "highly motivated" children: it was a college prep magnet in disguise.

I mention this bit of personal history because it illustrates a typical movement from "activist" parent to "consumer" parent, from wanting an active say or deliberate involvement in the programs to finding a suitable program one can at least live with. After all, involvement takes energy and after one's employment, other community involvements, and the rigors of home life—all of these often shared by both spouses—one has little remaining energy to help run the school.

This consumer mindset is virtually the norm in our culture and has had its impact on Highland. Consumer parents, though involved with Highland as they must be if it is to survive, nevertheless are different in outlook from the earlier activists. They contribute their energy to the program as long as they benefit from it. Of course the activists (and they are still present) also benefit; I am speaking of a matter of emphasis. Consumers have a more personal stake; activists are more oriented toward Highland's impact on the neighborhood or the welfare of all the children.

The Client Attitude

A third type of parent attitude arises out of the experience of poverty. Highland has always deliberately included low-income families because of its ethos and also because, as a neighborhood school, it was in a low-income area. The pressures of being poor, however, can create a beaten-down outlook, a feeling that "my life is out of control and I can't do anything about it." A significant number of parents at Highland have been young, single, minority women who have suffered from a sense of isolation in their struggle to bring up their children in a depressing neighborhood. Not far removed from childhood themselves, they approached Highland as a social service, seeking help for their children, like East German mothers photographed before the fall of the Berlin Wall handing their children across a border they themselves could not cross, pleading for a better life for these youngsters at least.

This last category of parents initially exhibits a clientlike attitude, a kind of dependency on those deemed more capable to take care of their children. This client orientation has been a huge obstacle that Highland's community has had to overcome. But Highland has grappled successfully with this problem, although it is ever present. At this point in Highland's development, probably as a result of its struggle to survive against great odds, the climate of the school nurtures the growth of activism among the clients and consumers. Everyone must put a shoulder to the load.

Thus three types of parent attitude toward involvement in the school are manifest at Highland, but the needs of the school are a magnet toward activism. Johnny Kimble, for example, consents to be board president for two years even though he no longer has children in the school. He gains a reputation as a tireless, dogged worker whether the activity be fund-raising or washing walls; and he is seen as a fair but demanding leader who collars other parents into helping out on necessary projects. Grace Renteria-Shirah has run the biweekly bingo operation for two years, a task requiring a minimum of ten evening hours a month on top of a full-time job. "Bingo is my thing," she smiles; her shrug at the listener's amazement belies her fatigue.

Shannon Hayes, Highland's first alumna parent, began as a stereotype of the clientlike parent; but she has evolved into something of an activist, even though she has not been able to contribute as mightily as the previous two. Initially she just wanted the best possible school for her children, although she had little idea what it would demand of her personally. Brenda DeWindt, who sent three of her children to Highland and became an assistant teacher, demonstrates a similar maturation.

The first two parents, Johnny and Grace, had a more middle-class background, and from their capacity to give more, approached Highland more from a consumer orientation than the latter two. Johnny and Grace understood from experience what "parent involvement" might entail, and they were capable of providing that leadership as long as they perceived that the school met their needs for good education for their children or others in the area.

The difference between initial client and consumer orientations probably originates in economic class, lower-income individuals being initially less interested in running the school, while middle-income persons are in a better position to trade skills and personal time (as well as money) for the benefits of Highland's program for their children. But the ethos of the school, its demand that all contribute in every way possible, soon disabuses the client-oriented and draws the consumer into taking ever larger responsibility.

The next section addresses the matter of how Highland *directly* and *formally* educates parents, through workshops and parent education nights. Following sections introduce the multiplicity of ways that parents can work in the school, organized by the Parent Coordinator, who is a staff person paid to structure and monitor all parent work in the school. I contend that such work also instructs parents in their interaction with their children at home, and the last section presents results of a survey of all parents in the 1994–95 school year to support that contention.

Educating Parents Formally

Highland teachers have always invited parents into the school for workshops on the Montessori method, but early in its history Highland began to address with the parents broader issues related to childrearing. Presented here are two vignettes, one of an all-school "retreat"-type meeting, conducted by outside professionals and aimed at surfacing parenting issues for group discussion, the other conducted by a Highland teacher to discuss alternative discipline techniques with three- and four-year-olds.

An All-School Parenting Workshop

The date is May 21, 1991, early in the evening. The cavernous but comfortable community room of Milwaukee's Neighborhood House (a neighborhood center about nine blocks west of the school) dwarfs two-and-a-half dozen adults seated in a circle for the evening's workshop on "Parent Oppression, Children's Liberation." About a third are males, about a third are minority, mostly African American. The leader is L.G. Shanklin Flowers, a dynamic African American woman in her early forties. She is assisted by an equally energetic Caucasian woman who is a public school counselor. Throughout the evening they take turns announcing activities and giving short homilies on parenting. The children of many of the parents are being cared for downstairs by two "at-risk" teenage girls. The child care has been arranged by Ranard Morris, the school's Parent Coordinator, and the term "at-risk" is his.

This meeting is the first all-school parent workshop of the year on the general topic of parenting. L.G. had led a workshop at the school about issues of racism and sexism earlier in the year. She was asked to return for this evening's meeting by the staff, who had enthusiastically enjoyed her last session. The Parent Board of Directors organized this event, and about 25 percent of the entire parent body volunteered to attend this Wednesday evening, but staff members seem disappointed with the turnout.

First, L.G. requests that every person give their name, their "family constellation" (e.g., married, divorced, single), why they came to the workshop, and what their chief concern about parenting might be. She begins by saying she decided at 37 years of age to bear a child who was now three and a half and whom she "co-parents" with her husband. She is here, of course, because she volunteered to conduct the workshop, and because she is concerned about how society oppresses parents and how parents in turn oppress their kids, all without being aware of the insidious process by which this oppression occurs. She will expand on this point later.

As each parent in the circle speaks up, an obvious atmosphere of sincerity, earnestness, and openness begins to develop. One recurrent theme is the struggle to "co-parent" when the couple is divorced or separated. About half the parents in the room are in this situation. Even more frequent is the expression of self-doubt about their skills as parents: "I want to do the best for my kids, but I'm not sure how." This, despite L.G.'s sincere acknowledgment at the outset that "everyone here is a very good parent." Some speak of their guilt at being too exhausted to spend the "quality time" with their children they feel they should.

Another frequent theme revolves around transferring their values to their children. Some Caucasian parents do not want their young sons to become "oppressive white males." African American parents want to shield their children from hurt in a racist society, yet want them to see everyone as an individual, not defined by the color of their skin. One Caucasian woman expresses concern about her adopted biracial child's identity development. An African American man expresses anger about his two kids growing up in (prejudiced) Milwaukee, and special upset at the likelihood that they would remain poor, with all that implied.

This interchange lasts nearly an hour, after which L.G.'s partner, Anita, summarizes the themes and speaks of the need for every parent to have a "support network," something society does not seem to value. Next, everyone pairs off to discuss in one-minute exchanges the following three questions. What do you appreciate about *your* parents? What do you appreciate about *yourself* as a parent? What do you appreciate about your children? L.G. asks people to share their thoughts after each exchange, and each time half a dozen different people speak directly and poignantly.

L.G. follows with a short lecture, as promised, on how parenting oppression functions. We are born, she begins, "powerful," ready to trust and grow. But as we hit bumps and are hurt along the way, we take on patterns of society as a reaction to being hurt. We become withdrawn or angry, for example. We carry this baggage, these patterns, into our adulthood, and then use them on our own children. We have to understand these inappropriate patterns and get rid of them if we are to allow our children to grow "naturally" through normal "discharges" (this term brought a few chuckles, which L.G. handled goodnaturedly), such as crying or temper tantrums, so they can heal rather than hide their hurt.

L.G. then gives the pairs five minutes each to talk about their own childhood baggage, their parenting story, or whatever they'd like. Each partner, in turn, is to listen with undivided attention, giving no advice, modeling how we should respectfully listen to our children and hear what they're really saying.

At the end everyone has a few moments to say what they liked about the session. All are positive, their appetites whetted for more such workshops in the coming school year. Many of these people do not know each other well. Some are complete strangers to others. But more links in the school community have been forged here this night. Ranard reminds those parents who have had child care to pay up before they leave. He collects about twenty dollars in cash to give his at-risk teenagers.

Parent Education Night

October 4, 1994. All the teachers and their assistants sit in their respective classroom areas waiting for parents to arrive at the designated 6:00 pm starting time. Sessions actually get under way about fifteen to twenty minutes later than that. Upstairs, Mary Ann Erdtmann devotes most of her remarks to her Junior Level curriculum, then opens the floor for discussion among the fourteen parents sitting in a circle.

The Children's House teachers start off in their respective areas, but Maribeth Pinkerton brings her very small gathering (about two parents) over to Tim's group after half an hour, swelling the number in the room to about fifteen parents. Some parents arrive later, others leave before the session is over. Tim focuses on two subjects, (1) the "absorbent mind" of the child as a preface to (2) nonpunishing disciplinary techniques. He gives examples of how a young child learns by "absorbing" and imitating adult behavior, then asks parents if they can think of examples. Several young mothers, some still in their teens, come up with excellent ones, such as a child crossing legs while sitting as Mommy does or "putting on my face" while playing with cosmetics.

Tim then passes out two sheets of paper, the first of which contains ways parents can teach phonetics at home (he does not speak to this paper). The second sheet contains numerous examples of alternative ways of speaking to children which explain and support rather than merely command. For example, instead of "shut up," try "I have to be able to hear Mary on the phone, so play more quietly please." The sheet also contains a poem entitled "Our Human Rights," which Tim uses to discuss how the teachers try to model good behavior in the classroom. Despite the presence of several small squirming children, the parents energetically discuss disciplinary situations with their children they wish to handle better. The meeting ends about 7:30 pm with Tim making announcements about upcoming school events for parents.

Although Highland's parent education program is "systematic," the reader should not infer that there is a program of parent "indoc-trination," bringing parents, especially poor ones, "up to speed" in parenting so they can be "on the same page" as the school. Such a view would be demeaning and arrogant. The term systematic means that parent education is a function of the very operation of the school, since it is, in effect, the parents' school. They run it, and have hired professionals—who are often school parents themselves—to help them. What would it mean for the self-image of public school edu-cators to see themselves as "support personnel" in the *parents'* school?

Nonetheless, as the vignettes showed, the school does have "parenting workshops," which are run by outside consultants, just as it has staff workshops for teachers and assistants, taking the view that everyone needs "inservice." Not every parent attends; some-times few parents attend. There is still staff irritation over some par-ents' resistance to their best efforts to involve them or help them in their parental struggles. Bob Desotelle, administrator until 1994, told me that about 20 percent of the parents don't do what is re-quired of them. I have heard discouraging talk from other staff and parents on occasion about Highland's shortcomings in dealing with the effects of poverty and racism on its families. But these com-ments ignored the successes, just as great athletes or performers will criticize their own performance about aspects the casual observer never noticed.

All Highland Parents Work in the School

Highland's "reaching the children through the parents" implies that Highland's policy is to educate parents as intensively and systemati-cally as it does the children. But the formal programs to educate parents are actually secondary to the education they receive by work-ing in the school regularly. Even if they are not exposed to adults modeling positive behavior with children during the day, concern for children's welfare is continually reinforced no matter what the work may be. If I am asked to paint a room in the school on a Saturday, for example, that sacrifice will remind me why I am doing it: ultimately at least for my child and certainly for the other chil-dren as well.

Some forms of parent involvement are very subtle, but they re-quire no less attention to the parent's awareness of his or her parenting role. For example, Highland's *Parent Handbook* points out that "a child's birthday is one of the most important events in the whole year." As part of the celebration the parents are asked to write a short biographical sketch of the birthday child. The *Handbook* continues:

If possible, we would like you to provide the derivation of the child's name, national origin, meaning, and why you chose it. And, if, for example, your child is having his/her fourth birthday, we ask you to provide a short paragraph for each year of life from birth to 1, 1 to 2, from 2 to 3 and from 3 to 4.

The *Handbook* offers examples of things to write about, information about what happens at the celebration, and suggestions for some other things for parents to provide, such as treats to share, pictures to accompany the biography, and of course the presence of the parents themselves.

It is worth devoting space, therefore, to describing the many ways Highland draws on its parents' support. The point person for involving parents is the Parent Coordinator.

The Parent Involvement Coordinator

In 1991 I interviewed Ranard Morris, a powerfully built African American man of thirty with an infectious smile and a pleasant manner. As the part-time Parent Involvement Coordinator of Highland Community School, he put in nearly a full day every day. First among his duties was tracking the hours of about sixty parent volunteers a month and helping them to find ways to fulfill their requirement of three hours a month. To this latter end, he organized parent workdays on weekends. A few days before the interview, for example, parents had transformed the mansion's former kitchen into an office for the Parent Involvement Coordinator which would serve double duty as a reception area for the school. A bathroom was added in a former pantry as part of this project and a couch placed near the door. As I chatted with Ranard, children passed in and out, either to use the bathroom, get playground equipment stored there, or to wait for friends or adults coming to pick them up at the nearby back door. He greeted them all by name. His office is situated at the crossroads of all traffic through the school.

Ranard's job also included coordinating the Bingo games that Highland runs in cooperation with several other nonprofit agencies twice a month. He ran an after-school recreation program for some Highland students whose parents couldn't pick them up until 5:30 pm, after work or their own classes had ended. (There was an extra fee for this service.)

During the rest of his "part-time" hours, this indefatigable organizer coordinated the teen work program. Eight "at-risk" teenage women were enrolled at Neighborhood House, the nearby community center, which contracted with Highland to have these young women do the school's housekeeping. They worked two-and-a-half hours a day two days a week after school. Neighborhood House had a grant to pay them minimum wage; Ranard supervised them. He also employed them to provide child care for all meetings at the school and for any parent who needed it while engaged in school activities. He collected the fees and paid the young women. Ranard also worked with the Parent Involvement Committee, which makes recommendations to the parent Board of Directors.

Asked his assessment of parent involvement at Highland, he said Highland is good at drawing parents in to participate in their kids' education. "We have the same kind of problem kids as the public schools," he continued. "The kids of the 90s have changed; most have not got a family structure. Our small size helps them to relate to an adult structure. A school with 700 kids in it couldn't do that. All they find there is anonymity." When asked to explain what he meant by helping kids relate to an adult structure, he said, "There are adults in each Highland child's school life who know them personally and who can function as mentors as well as teachers."

Ranard's position is pivotal for developing parent leadership. He is the one staff person in regular contact with all the parents in the school. He sees who shows potential for leadership and who does not. If schools are serious not only about involving parents but also about developing parent leaders, there will have to be a position like Ranard's.

By the 1994–95 school year, the Parent Involvement Coordinator job had expanded to three-quarters time and then into a full-time position by adding a quarter-time job as Maintenance Supervisor. Pat Farrington was the first to hold this full-time position, and by then the Afterschool Program had hired its own part-time director.

The Parent Involvement Contract

In order to register a child at Highland, each parent must sign a contract with the school which commits them to 36 hours of participation "in various activities" throughout the school year. Two-parent families therefore commit to a 72-hour minimum. The contract reads further:

> *Among those hours all parents are required to:*
> 1. *Attend two parent-teacher conferences each year for each child.*
> 2. *Meet at least once with the Parent Involvement Coordinator or member of the Parent Involvement Committee.*
> 3. *Work at least six (6) bingo events for single parent or twelve (12) for two parent family.*
>
> *Remaining hours may be completed by committee work, maintenance, child care, playground help, etc. . . . The Parent Board of Directors may give individual approval to exchange activities based on demonstrated personal needs. . . . Unless hours are completed prior to August 1, registration for the following school year may not be permitted.*

The contract form continues with a checklist of areas where parents can begin helping out. Parents can sign up to assist in the classroom, lunchroom, and/or playground. They can do office work, such as filing, letter addressing, or stuffing envelopes, or committee work on one of the standing committees. They can offer child care during bingo or parent events; and of course they can assist in maintenance of the physical plant and grounds. They may not become parent Board Directors, however, until they have been members of the School Corporation, the legal entity that is the Highland School, for at least two months.

The second sheet of the contract form lists and explains eight standing committees; each parent is asked to indicate their first, second, and third choices. The Parent Involvement Coordinator places each parent on at least one committee, chosen from the following:

- *The Parent Involvement Committee* coordinates parent work in school events which require significant parent labor. According to the *Handbook*, it encourages "the participation of parents within the school in a variety of ways."
- *The Fund-raising Committee* plans and coordinates fund-raising events which involve other parents, friends of Highland, and trustees.
- *The Finance Committee* develops and monitors the yearly school budget.
- *The Personnel Committee* monitors staff development, supervision, and evaluations; it recommends salary and benefit changes; and it hears any staff grievances. The *Handbook* states that it is "to act as advocate for the staff, and to facilitate communication between the staff and the Parent Board of Directors."
- *The Longrange Planning Committee* conducts long-range planning (for three years ahead) and develops strategies to implement these plans.
- *The Nurturing and Education Committee* seeks to "monitor and implement educational and nurturing programs for students, parents, boards, and staff."
- *The Operations Committee* exists to "monitor and develop building improvements and repair."
- *The Admissions Committee* determines classroom openings and interviews families applying for enrollment in Highland's programs.

If the prospective Highland parents have not experienced sticker shock yet about the time they will have to commit, the third page of the contract deals a further eyebrow-raiser: Each parent must "promise to sell (at least) a minimum amount of fund-raiser products or items. . . ." The four fund-raisers are the Autumn Dance, Cheese-cake Sales, Citrus Sales, and the Spring Raffle. For each event, sample point totals are given; for example, selling two tickets to the Autumn Dance nets the seller one point. Each parent must accumulate a minimum total of 32 points during the school year if the child is to be able to register for the next school year.

Highland's requirements for parent involvement are obviously demanding. In what ways do the parents respond? The following section analyzes the results of a survey of the parent body during the 1994–95 school year. The survey asked about family structure and demographics, ways parents had become involved at school, and a number of questions about their interaction with their children at home.

Survey of Highland Parents, 1994

Surveys were mailed in October to the 55 families who had enrolled children at Highland for the 1994–95 school year. Thirty-nine (71 percent) were returned. Twenty-five of the 27 two-parent families responded (93 percent); only 14 of the 28 one-parent families returned surveys (50 percent).

Socioeconomic Data on Highland Families

Twenty families indicated a family income of $35,000 or more. Sixteen families said they made $30,000 or less, seven of them saying it was $10,000 or less. Chapter 1 revealed that 28 of Highland's 68 students qualified for free lunches, two for reduced price lunches. Asked for the level of the mother's education, 13 said they had more than four years of college; only 5 responses said high school only. Eighteen had "some college," including technical school. Nineteen of the 39 mothers were Euro-American, 20 were minority. This information corroborates other evidence that Highland's parent body combines middle-class, working-class, and very low-income families. The educational levels of the mothers who responded were unexpectedly high, although half the single parents did not respond to the survey.

Types of Parental Involvement at Highland

Table 5.1 presents the frequencies of various parental involvement activities at the school. The frequencies were by family rather than individual parent, and could represent activities engaged in during the two months of the 1994–95 school year and the previous year. The figures are probably low since two respondents did not check any of the activity spaces, even though they had worked some hours at the school.

Table 5.1 Frequencies of Parent Activity at Highland
(in percentages, N = 39)

Parent Board of Directors	25.2%
Parent Involvement Committee	15.9%
Fund-raising Committee	13.3%
Finance Committee	8.0%
Personnel Committee	18.3%
Longrange Planning Committee	10.7%
Nurturing and Education Committee	15.9%
Operations Committee	8.0%
Admissions Committee	8.0%
Parent Education Workshops	42.0%
Classroom Help	47.5%
Lunchroom Help	18.6%
Playground Help	29.1%
Office Work	23.8%
Child Care	21.2%
School Maintenance	39.6%
Bingo Events	89.3%
Fund-raiser Sales	78.8%
Parent Conferences	92.0%
All-School Meetings	65.7%

One quarter of the respondents said they had served on the parent Board of Directors within the last two years. Nearly half had been active in Highland's classrooms. One in five had helped in the lunchroom, the office, or with child care, nearly one in three on the playground. Two in five had helped with school maintenance. Nearly all had attended parent conferences, and almost half had attended parent education workshops. Two in three had gone to all-school meetings. Almost everyone had participated in the mandatory bingo events and fund-raiser sales.

Highland Parents' Educational Involvement at Home

The questionnaire asked respondents to rate their involvement in home activities related to their children's education. The activities on the questionnaire, all culled from the literature on parent involvement, were the following:

1. hours per day the child watched TV
2. number of the child's friends whose parents the respondent knew
3. frequency with which the parent read to the child
4. frequency with which the parent talked with the child about what the child had written or read in school
5. involvement of the child in educational activities outside the school
6. frequency of contact with the child's Highland teachers

Notable frequencies were the following. About 35 percent of the parents said their children watched less than an hour of TV a day; nearly 22 percent said between one and two hours per day. Sixty percent said that they knew the parents of ten or more of their children's friends. More than half read to their child daily, and 28 percent more read to them two or three times a week. Eighty percent talked to their children every day about what they read or wrote in school. Fifty percent talked to their child's teacher daily; another 40 percent weekly. In-home parental involvement in their children's education is clearly substantial for Highland's parents. Their out-of-home activities with their children, despite requiring greater energy and resources, are also considerable. Table 5.2 shows the frequencies of parental involvement of children in educational activities outside school time. Under the category of "Other," parents included the Marquette Reading Program (a cooperative arrangement between Highland and Marquette University's College of Education to tutor

Table 5.2 Parental Involvement of Children in Educational Activities Outside School Hours (frequencies in percentages, N = 39)

Music Program	21.2%
Computer Camp	2.5%
Museum Trips	65.7%
Art Program	13.3%
Dance Program	15.9%
Multicultural Program	36.7%
Foreign Travel	10.4%
Other	29.1%

students in reading), swimming lessons at Marquette, "vacations out of town," "working with the mentally ill," trips to other states and cities, "library, travel overnight, zoo," "French class, drama class," soccer, "college for kids at UWM [University of Wisconsin-Milwaukee]," "math and reading camp."

Parental Attitudes Toward Highland

All but three of the 39 parents strongly agreed that their children had learned academically at Highland what they "should have learned by this time." Eighty-four percent strongly *dis*agreed with the statement "My child has not learned good social behavior at Highland." Responses were more mixed on whether the parents had learned new ways to handle their children's misbehavior since they had been enrolled at the school. Thirty-one of the 39, however, either tended to agree or strongly agreed, implying they felt Highland's ways of nurturing children had been models for them in some way. Thirty-three of 39 said their children liked attending Highland very much.

There were no statistical relationships, however, between the hours that parents put in at the school and any of the measures of parental involvement with their children in the home. The hypothesis that the more frequently parents worked in the school, the higher would be their scores on the parental-involvement-with-children measures was not validated. However, it should be noted that every parent did work in the school and that they gave considerable evidence that being in and around the daily operations of the schools did educate them, whether formally or informally, in ways to better interact with their children.

Some comments from the surveys returned are worth quoting: "We are crazy about the family/community aspects of Highland." "Highland is a place that provides a wonderful atmosphere for my child (not only academically, but socially as well), *and* it trained me to be an involved parent. In part, due to my experience, I chose to go into teaching." "There should be more Highland Community Schools in our world today. The world would be a better place!" "Highland is a great school, and my child loves being there."

The last section of the survey asked parents to check reasons why they sent their children to Highland. Table 5.3 lists frequencies of response to the categories presented.

Table 5.3 Frequencies of Reasons Cited for Sending Children to Highland (in percentages, N = 39)

Cultural Diversity	97.2%
Its Values	92.0%
Small Size	86.7%
Opportunities for Parent Involvement	86.7%
Its Faculty and Staff	78.8%
Its Academic Program	76.2%

Several mentioned the proximity of the school to their homes as another reason; two mentioned the academic curriculum.

Summary

The chapter identified three types of attitudes toward their own involvement with regard to the school that Highland parents have shown: activist, consumer, and client orientations. The school's demands for parent leadership draw the consumer- and client-oriented toward activism, a practical sense of responsibility that draws leadership even from some of the most unlikely candidates.

Highland educates parents as parents both formally through workshops and informally by its various requirements for work in the school. After discussing the role of the Parent Coordinator, the chapter listed these requirements for parent work in the parent contract.

A survey mailed to each Highland child's family asked parents about their family profile, their activities at the school, and ways they interacted with their children regarding educational matters. Seventy-one percent of the families responded. The data received corroborated other information about Highland's diverse family make-up, although a disproportionate number of single parents did not respond. Data from Highland showed that every parent worked in the school and that virtually all met minimum requirements for hours. Most, however, worked far more hours than the minimum, several putting in between one hundred and two hundred hours during the first eight months of the 1993–94 school year.

The measures of educational interaction with their children, such as monitoring TV-watching, reading and talking to them about reading, knowing the parents of their friends, contact with their teachers, and involving them in educational activities outside school hours all gave high scores to a majority of the parents responding. Most indicated that they had learned new ways to handle their children's misbehavior because they were involved at the school. The prime reasons given for sending their children to Highland were its cultural diversity, its values, its small size, and its opportunities for parent involvement. Its academic reputation and its faculty were also important attractions. The next chapter examines the issue of parents governing the Highland school.

Chapter Six
Parents Govern Highland

I really love Highland. It sort of feels like one big slightly dysfunctional family at times.

Parent on Highland's
Board of Directors

Highland is governed by the nine-member parent Board of Directors elected from the current body of parents. The parent Board has full legal responsibility for all decisions relating to the operation of the school. It sets and monitors the budget, makes and amends all school policies, hires and fires staff, and, in conjunction with principal and teachers, determines the curriculum. By every account, this governance arrangement has been successful and is a foundation stone of "parent-centeredness" at Highland. Highland's experience demonstrates that parent governance of a school can be a critical factor in building school effectiveness.

Parent governance of a school is the ultimate parent involvement strategy. By itself, it will not bring complete reform to public schooling. But it is a powerful tool to develop parent leaders, who in turn will reach out to other parents and draw them in. Parents will be motivated to become such "hounders," as one Parent Coordinator at Highland referred to herself, to the extent they themselves feel *responsible* for the enterprise of the school. By definition, parent governance is the ultimate condition to induce in them this sense of responsibility.

The fundamental rationale for such governance is that it can accomplish two goals. First, it promotes the involvement of other parents in their children's education. Second, it also benefits student learning when, in conjunction with teachers and staff, it places decision making about instruction and other matters that affect it close to the children, allowing the greatest responsiveness to the context.

Parent governance, complete or shared with administrators, is not a new idea. It falls under a larger concept, aimed at devolving power away from huge centralized public school bureaucracies and experimented with in a number of ways in recent decades. This chapter focuses on parent governance at Highland, with recommendations for public education. It begins, however, with a brief overview of these earlier experiments to make schools more autonomous, with the view that mere administrative decentralization does not necessarily empower parents at all and that giving parents full power and responsibility without other necessary changes, such as training, consultation, and full economic support, is simplistic. There follows a brief history of parent control at Highland, which includes comments from parent leaders during those years about their involvement and that of other parents. A survey of Highland's parent Board members for the 1994–95 school year closes the chapter.

Recent Experiments to Reform Decision Making in U.S. Schools

Site-Based Management

Site-based management was first designed and implemented on a district-wide basis in the 1980s in Dade County (Greater Miami) by Superintendent Joseph Fernandez, but attempts to place control of individual schools in the hands of those on site have a longer history, going back to the tumultuous 1960s and before (Williams, 1989). Decentralization of the largest urban school systems foreshadowed today's widespread demand for a greater share in school decision making. Many of the decentralization plans sought to give greater authority to principals, as in Los Angeles during the decade of the 1960s, but one plan sought deliberately to place parents in the dominant decision-making role.

New York City's Decentralization of Public Schools

In the mid-1960s the Ford Foundation sponsored an experiment to place several schools in some of New York's poorest neighborhoods under what was termed "community control" (Havighurst, 1979). Parents, as well as other community members, having been elected "by the community," would form a school's board of control. New York's huge system was ultimately segmented into 32 districts under the direction of elected Community School Boards (CSBs), but not before the CSB in the Ocean Hill–Brownsville area collided with the teachers' union over the CSB's sudden firing of several teachers and the principal of P.S. 201. The fallout from this notorious battle was that the power of the Community School Boards thereafter was severely curtailed. They could hire the district superintendent and later principals as well, but they could function only in an advisory capacity on budget and curriculum matters. And since the population of each district was between 200,000 and 300,000, the "localness" of each CSB was analogous to that of a board in a medium-sized city, with perhaps 50 to 75 schools to oversee.

One of the districts in New York City has become a national model for school choice, Harlem District #4. This example is often trumpeted as the triumph of choice, but it could just as well be used as an example of the effectiveness of devolving power away from the central board and toward the individual schools. Despite District #4's successes and national reputation, however, it later ran afoul of the central board. And many of the other districts have seen more than their share of corruption and power politics (Rogers and Chung, 1983).

Experiments giving more control to local school staffs and parents have become more drastic as urban school systems have deteriorated further. Two experiments are notable because they have been in existence long enough for some preliminary results to have filtered out: the Chicago Local School Councils (LSCs) and the Kentucky Educational Reform Act (KERA).

Chicago's Local School Councils

In the school year of 1990–91, after the Illinois Legislature had passed the enabling legislation, the Chicago School Reform Act of 1988, the entire school system of the city of Chicago, enrolling 410,000 students, was converted to a community-based governance approach. Before this plan went into effect the central board made all policy decisions, and principals, who were appointed with lifetime tenure by the central board, ran the schools. Each of the city's 540 public schools was to be governed by a ten-member elected council consisting of six parents with children in the school, two teachers at the school, and two community residents without children at the school. These Local School Councils (LSCs) could:

1. hire the principal and negotiate a four-year contract with him or her
2. specify the school's educational goals
3. approve the curriculum and a plan to raise academic achievement
4. make recommendations on teachers and teaching materials.

During the first year of the LSC experiment political struggles heated up everywhere, but achievement scores did not budge. The board and many principals, 84 percent of whom were retained by the LSCs, foot-dragged on proposals for change, especially because the system was weighed down by a $316 million deficit. Another problem, to have been expected, was that the LSC members, teachers as well as parents, were unprepared to take on governance responsibilities. As a result there was factional fighting within LSCs as well as between LSCs and their staffs at the schools. Many council members were demoralized, one-third of them indicating in a *New York Times* poll that they "definitely would not" run again for a two-year term after their current term was up in November, 1991 (*New York Times*, June 30, 1991, pp. 1, 11). Yet council stability is crucial to the success of this reform effort.

Three years later an evaluation of Chicago's school reform reported that on the three outcomes specified in the legislation, that is, improved reading and math scores, improved attendance and improved graduation rates, the schools still had shown no improvement (Walberg & Niemiec, 1994). The percentage of students scoring at or above national norms on reading and math actually declined a bit over three years. Attendance rates remained about the same during that period, but graduation rates from high school also declined slightly. On the other hand, a survey of 13,500 teachers and principals mentioned in the same article found that a majority felt the schools were getting better as a result of the reforms. And a survey of several thousand members of LSCs, also in the same article, found that 68 percent felt their schools performed better than during the previous year.

Thus far the Chicago reform effort seems to show that students are not achieving better, although most of the teachers, principals, and council members think well of their own accomplishments. I suggest that this experiment is not nearly radical enough to work; it has changed *only* the power relations, a necessary but obviously not sufficient condition for school improvement. The next reform movement discussed, the Kentucky Educational Reform Act, or KERA, embodies the same intent with regard to local control, but is much more comprehensive in nature.

The Kentucky Educational Reform Act (KERA) of 1989

Kentucky's supreme court in 1989 found that the state's public schools were inequitably funded and that therefore the state's educational system was unconstitutional. In response the state legislature enacted a comprehensive plan to reform the entire school system. Major elements of the legislation were the following:

1. The elementary schools, at least the first three grades, were to be ungraded.
2. The curriculum was to become oriented toward active learning and cooperative problem solving. Assessment was to move away from standardized paper and pencil testing.
3. Schools were to be held accountable: if teachers met the state-imposed goals, they could receive a salary increase of up to one-third; if not, they could lose tenure.
4. There were to be new technologies employed in the classroom, and family and preschool resource programs were to be started.
5. Funding was to be equalized across districts.
6. Decisions were to be made at the school level.

An even more important mandate for the present discussion was that each school was to form a council by 1996 with the authority to set policy in eight areas: curriculum, staff time, student assignment, schedule, school space, instructional issues, discipline, and extracurricular issues. Each council was to be composed of the principal, two teachers, and three parents elected by their peers.

The first two years of a five-year study, done even before KERA had been fully implemented, indicated that school-based decision making "has been a major force in communicating the seriousness of KERA across the state and a critical link between schools and their communities" (David, 1994, p. 707). The study found that in the nearly 50 percent of the schools that had established councils by 1993, most teachers were happy to be able to select their principals and many parents were glad to have an official voice in school policy-making.

Participation by all parents was dismally low, however; the most optimistic estimate of eligible parents actually voting was 22 percent. Teacher participation, in willingness both to run for a seat on the council and simply to vote, has been difficult to achieve as well, especially among younger elementary teachers. Other findings showed that thus far the principal determines the council's style of operation. Principals accustomed to sharing power were more likely to have effective councils than authoritarian principals, who tended to make council members feel powerless. Council members needed training in group process skills and being effective representatives. They needed skills in setting agendas, soliciting input from their larger constituencies, holding efficient meetings, delegating authority, and feeding back information to others, as well as in avoiding "personal agendas" in public meetings.

The study investigated how the formation of the councils contributes to the transformation of curriculum and instruction in ways that improve student performance. Thus far changes in curriculum and instruction—which were in fact occurring and in the directions intended by KERA—seemed to be due more to the new primary program and outside consultants who work with individual schools than to decisions made by the councils. In fact, a frequent complaint from council members was that the staff does not implement their decisions, whether because the principal was unwilling or because they themselves have not "done their homework" necessary to make their case and build broad support for their decisions. I infer, from the study's lack of mention of how all parents are systematically involved, that in fact little attention has been paid to this essential precondition for successful parent governance. Furthermore, little mention is made in the study of how councils relate to the body of parents and teachers—other than sometimes not "doing their home-work" regarding decision making.

These complaints remind us that the ultimate purpose of a lo-cal school council is to advance student learning. The intent is to put decision making about curriculum and instruction, and other matters that affect them, as close to the children as possible to allow for flexibility and responsiveness to context. In order for this deci-sion making to be effective, therefore, it must be truly representative and open to sharing power. As the councils in Kentucky are discov-ering, there is much yet to learn, and the implications of this radical restructuring for everyone involved are only gradually beginning to become clear.

One more approach to reform, charter schools, which have been legislated for in several states, should be mentioned before discuss-ing parent decision making at Highland.

Charter Schools

Charter school legislation in states that have begun to enact it seeks to promote school decision making and innovation at the individual school level by enabling state funds to go directly to each school with little or no district oversight in the crucial areas of budget su-pervision, the placing, development, and transfer of teachers and principals, and the determination of the curriculum. In effect, par-ents, as well as teachers and other professional staff, can start their own schools and receive public funds from the state with minimal involvement by their local districts. For example, in 1993 the Michi-gan Legislature passed a bill enabling certain groups to form their own schools and apply to the State Department of Public Instruc-tion for a "charter" (a statement of purpose given official sponsor-ship by the state). The purpose of the legislation was to encourage innovative programs by allowing them to operate independently of districts. Approval requires conformity to minimal state standards and entitled the school to full reimbursement, on a per student ba-sis, from state coffers.

Legislators hoped that by limiting application to groups with educational affiliations, they might avoid the more unusual forms of schooling which might crop up. But the first group to apply for a charter was the Noah Webster Academy, a statewide consortium of homeschoolers, primarily religious in their motivation, who sought to create a statewide computer network whereby children could do their studies "long distance" through interactive programming. Officials of the Noah Webster Academy, based in Ionia, Michigan, admitted that parents, most of whom are not certified teachers, would be the children's primary instructors. Although Noah Webster was granted a charter, members of the State Board of Education initiated a successful lawsuit to stop them from receiving state funds on the grounds that the state would be funding religious education (Foren, 1994).

The principal issue in charter schools, however, is oversight and accountability. In Kentucky the individual districts continue their supervisory function, although the state has mandated the changes they must follow. In Michigan and in other states chartering schools, the supervision of these schools occurs at the state level, a greater distance, although the expectation is that each school will conform to minimum state standards. Court rulings on suits brought by opponents of charter schools, however, have required more emphasis on public accountability where private funds are expected. In Michigan, for example, in November, 1994, Ingham County Circuit Court Judge William Collette ruled Michigan's charter schools unconstitutional so that none of the ten of them in existence could receive state funds. Just before Christmas, legislators rewrote the law to enable funding.

The judge's concern was the issue of oversight. If schools receive public funds, they should be accountable to the public. A strong central authority exercises a watchdog function to prevent patronage (e.g., getting the board president's sister hired as the principal). It also defines common goals and standards while allowing local schools to find innovative ways to reach these goals (Shanker, 1994a). The Michigan experiment is still too young to determine what abuses will arise. But they will arise, and having the oversight function so far removed from the site guarantees that they will be serious by the time the machinery of accountability gets up to speed.

The charter school concept may be one of the most radical reforms in modern education, primarily because it undermines district supervision and control. Proponents see its potential to innovate and to involve parents and teachers deeply in governance; sincere opponents not only may be fearful of change but also worry about the potential abuses of devolving power to such an extent. While it is much too soon to determine whether the charter school's advantages will outweigh its disadvantages, the risks are worth taking as long as adequate public oversight can be developed. One proposal for such control bears study, that of electing school boards as a slate (Schlecty & Cole, 1993). Rival slates would run on a platform (the proposal calls it a "charter," but platform carries the notion without confusion), which would be a detailed description of long-term goals and strategies for the entire school district. Schools within these districts could still innovate autonomously, as the KERA schools are doing. The "charter school board" idea preserves democratic control while tilting the balance away from politics and toward education.

Highland's experience in school governance gives another perspective, one from the inside. Several Highland parent leaders speak of their experience on parent participation and governance as it developed at the school. The results of a survey of Highland's 1994–95 parent Board of Directors follows this discussion.

Parent Control at Highland

As the foregoing descriptions of reform experiments in local control make clear, simply announcing that parents will have the majority of votes in policy-making for the school guarantees nothing. Power sharing, particularly among populations not used to participating in "the system," requires meticulous and difficult preparation, often taking years to accomplish. The cooperative working relationships attested to below by principal Tim Souers in Highland's Spring 1993 newsletter are the result of two decades of bringing parents into partnership with the educators in the school. The following excerpt from Tim's article "Working for Parents" exemplifies this partnership process:

Recently I went before the parent board to ask for a one year sabbatical from my principal duties. After discussing some of their thoughts, they asked a simple question: "What does this mean to the quality of education for our children?"

I was directed to prepare a plan in one month explaining how the school could best handle the situation without any disruption to the students' education. At first I was taken aback. I had wanted parents to deal with the problem, but they knew that they did not have the expertise.

When I took this directive back to the faculty, I realized once again the wisdom of empowering parents to run their school. The staff and I brainstormed and came up with some very creative and exciting options for the next year. Options that in some ways created more work for all of us, but ones that we all agreed to because of the growth possibilities for us as educators. When I took this new job-specific proposal back to the personnel committee of the board, they were supportive and currently the board is implementing its plan for filling this position.

Respect and accountability within the educational work place are often conflicting principles. Many teachers report a striking feeling of a lack of respect from parents and society in general. Many parents report feelings of powerlessness and a lack of any accountability from their child's school.

These feelings do not exist at Highland.

What does exist at Highland is a hard working and serious spirit of cooperation between parents and staff. I cannot say that it always works as well as in my example, but I can say that I have grown to believe that it is one of the essential missing elements for effectively educating our nation's children.

A Brief History of Highland's Board of Directors

Highland's original incorporation papers put the number of directors at seven, five parents with children currently in the school and two staff, including the administrator, ex officio. As I recall, our first board had only three parents, due to the lack of willing candidates and lack of interest in the election. Those three parents meant well but basically left all decision making to the staff. By the time I left the school five years later in 1974, I remember feeling that the curriculum was much further developed than parent participation on the Board of Directors.

In fairness to those parents, I had done little to cultivate their involvement, whether by the myriad ways they are now required to contribute their time in the school or by training parents in the skills necessary to function as agents of control. I had simply assumed that parent involvement meant that parents would take the reins of the school without realizing the many steps required to bring them to that point.

In 1977 a parent who was also a VISTA volunteer, Phyllis Kimble, became the school's first Parent Coordinator. She started the Parent Involvement Committee of the Board. "When I came in," she said,

some single parents were not being asked to do anything in the school, but I thought that was wrong. Everyone, including single parent poor people, should be required to do. We needed stability in the program; we needed a staff person to be the Parent Coordinator. I got tough as the Parent Coordinator; I even asked some parents to leave the school.

As the 1980s began, parents were still actively welcomed into the school, but the idea of making considerable demands on every parent had begun to take shape in policy form, administered by a formal Admissions Committee. Ellen Pizer-Kupersmith, a former administrator and parent at Highland during this period, echoed this view.

I saw Highland as a place for parents to socialize; but a school should have real *things for parents to do. I would call and invite them to get involved. Whereas public school parents feel threatened by their school, Highland has always attracted people who were willing to give everything.*

Not everyone was so willing, however. A Parent Coordinator of the late 1980s spoke to the universal and eternal problem of the conflict between those who do more and those who do less:

Getting parents to fundraise is the hardest part; out of 45 families, only ten did Bingo regularly. We need to enforce sanctions against parent deadbeats because it upsets the working parents.

Johnny Kimble, former president of the Board of Directors in the mid-1980s—*after* his two children had left Highland—was one of Highland's many demanding yet self-sacrificing leaders.

I would never allow the use of the word can't. I wanted to see a mix on the Board of educated and uneducated parents; I pushed people to contribute, even to washing toilets, because kids will see this and respect them for showing such a high investment in them. There was a bureaucratic structure at Highland, but everyone was represented. So even though decisions took a long time, longer than I might have wanted, everyone was invested.

This relentless push for involvement of each parent at every level has laid the foundation for the involvement of parents at the highest levels. Brenda DeWindt, an assistant teacher in the Junior Level in 1989 and single mother of three sons at Highland, spoke of her introduction to Highland.

My first interview with the Admissions Committee scared me; I'd never heard such demands being made on parents. I tried to do what I was asked, but the first year was slow because I didn't know what I was doing. I sewed dust covers for the old ditto machines and did other work around the office. I worked on Bingo, went on day trips with the kids, helped in the lunchroom, and I even taught some lessons in the classroom. I ran for the board and served three years, and I'll run again. In the beginning I didn't feel qualified to do things. I was scared, especially as a substitute teacher. But Tim told me to listen to the kids. And I learned. Highland is for the parents, too. I've come a long way because of Highland.

Highland is a community which has demanded much of its parents, but it has supported them as well. Here are the voices of some other parents who were brought into Highland's community and who thought of themselves as having learned a great deal in the process. Eniola Oladeji, an assistant teacher, first in the Children's House and then in the Junior Level, and a single parent of three former Highland students, spoke of her involvement with Highland over more than a decade.

I am an example of a parent who was educated toward positive parenting skills. I was encouraged to advance my own education, and I had the opportunity to serve and develop my skills at Highland. I've learned to voice my opinions, though I'm a quiet person, because meetings are in a

*supportive environment. There is a buddy system here for parents. High-
land won't let you slip through the cracks.*

Indeed, the Highland community's concern often has extended
to those who had long before left the school. Highland's first alumna
parent, Shannon Hayes, was a single mother with two sons at Highland in 1989.

*Brandon was born when I was fifteen. I did drugs and dropped out of
school, but Highland people kept after me, knowing my mother, and got
me to finish high school. Now I want a degree in computers at MATC
[Milwaukee Area Technical College]. I help serve lunch and go on field
trips, picnics, and swimming lessons, and I help out in the classroom.
The kids all look up to me when I come in; that's good for Brandon and
Demetrius. Highland taught me not to give up.*

Pat Farrington was the Parent Coordinator in the 1993–94 school
year on a three-quarters time basis. As the liaison with Highland's
fifty-five families, she referred to herself as "chief hounder." Her job
included monitoring parent hours for the 81 names on her parent list,
setting up home visits, "hustling" new parents for the parent Board of
Directors, and being the person riding herd on bingo and other parent fund-raising activities. She calculated that parents had contributed 3,465 hours for the first eight months of that school year. But
she made it "as easy as possible" to get those hours: "We give parent
hours for everything. Even going to meetings qualifies for hours."

Long after parent involvement in the school was established,
the Board of Directors expanded to nine members, all parents. The
rigorous demands for participation over the years had surfaced competent leadership from every sector of the parent group. The school
was ready to be the parents' school in fact as well as mission. And
now, as each new family enters the school, the informal training for
leadership begins, supported by the infrastructure, the expectations,
experiences, policies, and practices carved out over the years to empower parents in their children's education.

Survey of Highland's 1994–95 Parent Board Members
A survey form was mailed to each of the nine parents of Highland

Board of Directors in late October, 1994. Seven of the nine members responded. The survey questions focused on each member's types of involvement at Highland before and during Board service and on assessment of the Board's skills at conducting meetings and interacting with its various constituencies (administration, teachers, parent body, trustees).

Length of Service

The average length on the Board of the seven respondents was two years. Five of them had joined the Board less than a year after first enrolling their child at Highland. I infer from this last statistic and from comments by the Parent Coordinator that pressure has to be exerted to take on Board responsibilities and that this pressure starts as soon as some parents become members at Highland. My own experience on a number of grass-roots neighborhood and community organization boards verifies that getting people to take on and stick with these jobs is difficult. So to find, in an organization whose parent base usually numbers less than 80, nine who will take on governance tasks, is unusual. I believe this large proportion is due to Highland's reputation preceding it; that is, anyone who applies and "passes" the Admissions Committee is probably already prepared to take on significant involvements, or at least knows they will be required to do so.

Types of Service by Parent Board Members

All but one of the respondents indicated that they had served on one or two of the standing committees, such that each committee had at least one parent Board member on it. Typically this service began with their enrollment of their children and continued after they became Board members. They had all attended parent education workshops, parent conferences, all-school meetings, bingo events, and done fundraiser sales. Five had volunteered in the classroom, four for child care, three for school maintenance work. Two each had volunteered for playground, lunchroom, or office help. One had chaired the parent letter writing campaign to raise money for the school.

Only one respondent had no previous outside experience to prepare for working as a parent Board member at Highland. Two had served as members of other agency boards in the community.

Six had served on committees in other organizations. Three had served on Highland committees before their Board service.

This information on previous service suggests that committee assignments can provide experience in handling formal group tasks, which parents in governance positions need. But it is instructive to note that six of the seven respondents had served on committees in other organizations. I infer from this finding that someone who has never served on a committee would be less likely to emerge in governance positions. Also, the more of the real functioning of the school they can experience, through volunteer work in classrooms, on the playground, in the lunchroom, on field trips, in office work, in building maintenance, and in fund-raising, the more understanding they can bring to their decision making. Since Highland demands all of these sorts of involvements, the school is by that very fact training potential Board members.

Assessments of Board Skills in Conducting Meetings

Three of the seven respondents strongly disagreed with the statement "Our current Board holds efficient meetings." The others tended to agree that they were efficient. Perhaps these mixed feelings could be summed up by one who wrote, "We need to move through the agenda faster, but some issues require more time than others." Asked whether the Board needed skill in setting and following meeting agendas, the average response was neutral, again indicating some dissatisfaction with the efficiency of the process. The majority, however, tended to disagree that some members of the Board were following their own "agendas." The putative inefficiency of the monthly Board meetings, however, did not seem to douse the enthusiasm of its members. All but one strongly agreed that they liked being on the Board, even though it was hard work.

Assessment of Board Skills in Interacting with Its Constituencies

The respondents expressed mixed feelings about the Board's ability (a) to solicit input from the parent body and from staff, (b) to delegate authority, and (c) to keep everyone informed about its decisions. That is, ratings of statements on these issues for the most part elicited neither strong agreement nor strong disagreement. I assume this means that members feel they can improve in these areas as a group. But as one wrote: "We're a group of parents, not professionals, doing the best we can. All in all, I think we do a pretty good job."

Responses about the Board's relationship with staff were among the most interesting in the survey. Asked to respond to the statement "The lines of authority are clear at Highland: the Board makes the decisions and the staff carries them out," four strongly agreed, two strongly disagreed, and one was neutral, entering the word "Ha!" next to the rating. This question was intended to uncover to what degree Board members took an authoritarian view of their role in decision making. Views therefore seemed mixed on this point, although one respondent wrote that this was a misleading question at Highland, meaning, I assume, that the Board-staff relationship is not so cut and dried. A follow-up statement probed the matter further by speaking to Board-staff conflict: "Whenever there is conflict between the Board and the staff, it is due to staff unwillingness to implement the Board's decision." Disagreement with this statement appeared quite strong. It is worth quoting two responses in particular. Here is the first:

Highland has a wonderful staff that deals daily with the frustrations of being underfunded. They do not suffer in silence and have many allies on the parent Board. As a Board member it takes incredible strength to balance the desire to approve funding for fine proposals brought to the Board by people they respect, along with the need to act responsibly with limited resources so that Highland avoids continued financial crisis or worse. There are times when as a Board member I feel manipulated by the staff. They need to be careful what they ask for because ultimately they are going to get it. That is a power and responsibility I don't believe the staff realizes it has.

The second response was this:

The HCS board is nontraditional in comparison to other boards I'm on, due in large part because our children are loved and educated at Highland. Though we understand our roles, it is not as cut and dried as other boards because we do know and interact with staff at all kinds of levels outside of our role as board members. I think it means we bring much more intimacy to our discussions and decisions. Highland is a very special community and given some of the tough decisions we're making, I believe we have a special board. I've been reluctant to be on the board given my starting my own business and the time required there, but I've been able to contribute my gifts as well as limit my involvement where necessary.

The Board respects the staff highly, though members wouldn't necessarily return to the early days when staff were Board members themselves. There was also consensus that the Board works reasonably well with the trustees; at least no one strongly disagreed. In general, Board members saw their role in a serious vein, as evidenced by written comments from two others.

I have been an involved Westside resident for 25 years and as a "second time around" parent of a preschool child, I'm ever grateful that HCS has thrived in these years and that I'm able to be a participant! My work on the Board is some of the best work I do in my life to actively support the diversity of our neighborhood and its importance in our children's life.

As a Board member I see us as caretakers of a great tradition. Besides presiding over administrative issues, we also listen for and state the consensus of all stakeholders, i.e., students, staff, parents, and friends, regarding our future direction as a positive force in Milwaukee.

Summary

The research literature on parental involvement in school governance and analysis of Highland's experience allow us to craft some guidelines for schools and districts contemplating such parental empowerment. The underlying assumption here is that parents will have *real* power, not merely advisory status. But changing *only* the power relations in the school is not enough.

Parental involvement (as with teacher involvement) in the school governance process requires preparation. Ultimately any local board member needs skills in working with others in the task group and an understanding of the entire operation that is being overseen. Skill in group dynamics can be taught for in workshops and practiced in committees and other practical task groups. Understanding of the multiple facets of the school can be gained by volunteering to work in them.

At the beginning of parent governance reforms, the first parents might be those with experience in committee or other board work and who have volunteered in the school before. The board will also need to develop skills in relating to its constituencies—the parent body, the staff, other community members (possibly trustees?), central office figures. They must learn to "do their homework" in thinking through and lobbying for any policies they wish to add or change. They will need courage to face the inevitable conflicts, both internal and external.

Parental involvement, especially at this level of responsibility, will have to be pushed. It won't happen spontaneously, for the most part. But as parents see the importance of taking charge of their children's school, they will become more willing to make the sacrifices necessary. Their commitment to the task will be a combination of this vision and the attractiveness of the group. By this latter I mean that the members enjoy one another's company to a degree, or at least are not put off by others' behaviors in the group.

On the matter of board composition, should a local board be composed of staff and parents or just parents? Highland's experience started with staff (a teacher and the administrator) sitting on the board, along with a majority of parents. As parents gained more confidence through the years, they no longer needed staff as voting members. This appears to have been a natural evolution over at least a decade. Initially, local boards will probably require such staff presence, but the ultimate goal is that staff not have to remain as board members.

Finally, parental governance is of a piece with reform of the total school. It does not drive it, as the Chicago experience is demonstrating. Parents should work with staff to encourage and support innovation in the classrooms and curricula. The entire parent body must be drawn into helping the school function. The ultimate guideline is always: what is best for the children? (though this question rarely admits of a simple answer). And of course, the principal and/ or instructional leader of the school must be facilitative in her relationships with the board, willing to share power. The next chapter discusses the role of the trustees of Highland, a unique feature of the school which may have implications even for publicly funded schools.

Chapter Seven
The Trustees of Highland

*The trustees measure success by Highland's parent involvement,
not only by the kids' test scores.*

Frank Miller, former trustee
and Highland parent

The trustees of Highland Community School form a loose-knit task group organized to help the school with fund-raising and technical expertise. They do not exert any formal authority over the school, although informally they exert influence because of their importance in the school's year-to-year existence. (I refrain from using the term *board* of trustees in order to avoid confusion with the parent Board of Directors, although some trustees and others in the school use the term, as well as "Trustee Board of Directors.")

This chapter first describes the historical evolution of the trustees as a group, a process which was a classic example of the "each one reach one" phenomenon. It then discusses the trustees' role in the school, which although informal is nonetheless essential to the school's continued existence. The chapter also analyzes results of a survey mailed to all the trustees and trustees emeriti during the fall of 1994, designed to elicit a profile of trustee involvement and attitudes. It ends with a discussion of the relevance of a trustee group for an urban public school.

A History of Highland's Trustee Group
In the first twelve years of the school's existence, the trustees were an aggregation of altruistic consultants from Milwaukee's business and legal communities upon whom the administrator could call for advice or help in solving particular problems. For example, I painfully

remember receiving a notice from the IRS in 1972, announcing that the school was 215 days late in filing Form 990 for tax-exempt organizations, and that at ten dollars a day, the penalty was $2,150. (In my naivete, I had thought that if we were tax-exempt, we didn't have to file anything further.)

That amount was more than we had in the bank. Panicked, I called attorney Mike Bolger, another "protector" figure in the school's history, who in turn placed a call to the IRS signatory in Philadelphia. After he explained my inexperience and the fragile nature of this grassroots enterprise, the penalty was waived pending quick receipt of Form 990.

I had met Mike when both of us were seniors at Marquette University in 1960. We had joined the Jesuit order together in 1961 and left several months apart in 1968. Mike had become an attorney in the next three years, then signed on with a large law firm in Milwaukee. Mike's interest ran deeper than merely intervening to get me out of scrapes with bureaucracies, and he urged several of his friends to become involved, including an accountant and a real estate appraiser. Mike began to call this group the board of trustees, though it had no formal status in Highland's corporate structure. In fact, in the current bylaws of the corporation (revised May, 1991), the word trustee is never mentioned.

Robert Weyerhaeuser, of the lumber company family, became interested in the school, hearing of it from a friend, who happened to be my brother-in-law. Robert ultimately became the major benefactor of the Highland School, supporting scholarships and capital expenditures, including the purchase of the building and the remodeling of the basement into a cafeteria. He continued his generous support for twenty-two years, acting as a trustee emeritus toward the end of his involvement. In several of those years his contributions made the difference in the school's meeting its budget.

Frank Miller, a parent at the school since 1973 and at the time a program director at a local neighborhood youth center, also became one of the first trustees and invited Byron Tweeton, an independent fund-raising consultant, to join the trustee group. Cathy Miller, at the time my office assistant at the school, invited her father, Dr. James Ghiardi, a professor in Marquette's Law School, to sign on.

In the 1973–74 school year Byron planned the first fund-raising campaign for the school, with the more-than-ambitious goal of collecting a million dollars over the next five years. I can vividly recall the small group of Highland leaders—a few staff, parents, and trustees—meeting at Frank and Cathy's house with Byron and Mike Bolger. Each couple (all had brought our spouses) met separately with Byron in the kitchen, where he softly urged us to pledge what were then incredible amounts of money to kick off the campaign. Ours was a five-year pledge of $1,800, increasing yearly (our total family income that year was $4,500). Byron's pitch was simply that the people who cared the most about the school had to lead the way for others by giving the most. When Mary Alice and I left the kitchen, we felt as though we had been mugged. But of course Byron was right. Scores of people, staff, trustees, and parents, have been making the same kind of sacrifices to make Highland work ever since.

In the 1980–81 school year Mike Bolger resigned as chair of the trustees, although he remained a trustee. Byron also pulled back considerably to devote more time to his other interests. Cathy Miller left as administrator. The response under Ellen Pizer-Kupersmith, Cathy's replacement, was to expand the trustee group, now chaired by Ed Makovec, an accountant who was to provide great stability to Highland by remaining as chair for the next seven years. The trustees grew in number to more than a dozen, although there has been a steady core who have remained from the earliest years and provided stability. Everyone is in agreement that without their fund-raising efforts (now about $100,000 a year) Highland would quickly sink into hopeless debt.

During the 1994–95 school year Highland officially listed thirteen members of the "Acting Trustee Board," two "Trustees on One Year Leave," and four members of the "Trustee Emeritus List." These individuals have come from a variety of organizations in the Milwaukee area. Some of these institutions are among the largest corporations in the country; others are much smaller enterprises created and headed by the trustee. Some are social service, educational, or municipal institutions. With the exception of Mike Bolger, who is now the president of the Medical College of Wisconsin, the trustees from the larger corporations tend to occupy positions in upper-middle management, close to but not at the top. For example, in his first year as the president of the trustee group is Walter E. Juzenas, the director of Distribution Services for Miller Brewing Company. The vice president of the trustees is Donald W. Layden, the executive vice president of M&I Data Services, Inc. Barbara Piehler, who acts as the trustee group's secretary and treasurer, is a vice president and assistant to the president of Northwestern Mutual Life Insurance. Others are attorneys, marketing specialists, accountants, educators. Virtually all have management experience, although in some cases their fund-raising experience is limited. Although they enjoy comfortable incomes, none of them would be considered wealthy.

Highland's trustees are a unique sector of the Highland community. They meet eleven times a year at the school and sometimes attend all-school functions, but many are quite distant sociologically from most of Highland's parents and staff, living in far-off suburbs (two trustees were also parents during the 1994–95 school year, however). Yet paradoxically they are fiercely committed to Highland's success. Sally Lewis, trustee chairperson during the 1989–90 school year and an attorney for Northwestern Mutual Life Insurance Company, spoke of taking pride in her involvement. Mike Bolger continues to view Highland as among his chief social causes. Their civic pride and concern for education find substance in the reality of Highland. But it is still hard to keep asking friends for money. "It takes great will," according to Frank Miller.

Trustee Mary Louise Mussoline, phased out as fund-raising consultant to the administrator in 1990 while still a Highland parent, demonstrated how cohesive is the bond between the trustees and the rest of the school. She cited trustees' willingness to raise money without conflict with the parent Board of Directors, who spend it. Trustees are thus not only those in whom the rest of the school trusts; they themselves trust the staff and especially the parents. "What is unique," Sally Lewis told me, "is the belief by the trustees that parents can run the school."

The Trustee Role

A memo to the trustees from Walter Juzenas, chair of the trustee group, dated July 22, 1994, spelled out the responsibilities of Highland's trustees. The primary responsibility of each trustee is fund-raising: "Each trustee is expected to raise $1,800 annually by participating in the letter campaign to individuals and small businesses," he wrote. And "each trustee will be matched with five corporations/ foundations to oversee the solicitation and management of the contact."

Second, each trustee is to donate "a minimum of $300 annually or provide alternative funding." Third, trustees are "encouraged" to attend monthly trustee meetings at the school and special committee meetings as they arise. A fourth but not less important responsibility of each trustee is to "advise and support" the school. This means a "willingness to share personal talents and knowledge in assisting the school and other board [trustee] members." Fifth, each trustee should serve "as ambassador to the community on behalf of Highland." And sixth, each trustee should serve a three-year term.

On May 4, 1994, I attended a special meeting of the trustees called over dinner at Milwaukee's Wisconsin Club to discuss the future of the trustee group. Attendance at meetings had been lagging and the trustees appeared to be several thousand dollars short of their fund-raising goal, leaving the school with a $9,000 deficit. There was not exactly a crisis atmosphere, but some of the trustees were concerned that the efforts of the group were not adequately supporting the school. Most of the trustees attended, a dozen, as well as the school's administrator, and Cindy Brown, the parent Board President.

Dan Johnson presided and asked each person to start off the session by stating why they had become trustees of the school. As each person spoke, it became clear their commitment to quality education for the community, as Highland provided it, was extremely important to them. Those with more fund-raising experience spoke of the need to get more "heavyweights" as trustees, individuals who could personally give a significant amount of money as well as get others they knew to do likewise. Mike Bolger cited a rule of thumb: "You usually get 85 percent of your funds from individuals, wealthy and otherwise, and 15 percent from foundations. Highland has this reversed."

But the evening was full of positive notes. Several spoke of the advantages for Highland the trustees represented. For example, the group members possessed a range of professional skills Highland could draw upon for free. Trustees had also helped Highland achieve financial stability. And indeed, each trustee demonstrated a strong spirit of commitment. The meeting ended with a promise of rededication in very specific ways by several trustees.

A Survey of Trustee Involvement and Attitudes

The trustee group is an important element of the school's existence, but it is also relatively invisible. So it bore further study beyond attending meetings or reminiscing. Accordingly, I mailed a questionnaire to every trustee and trustee emeritus during the fall of 1994, asking them to list their corporate position, who recruited them, and the number of their years of service to Highland. They were asked then to check off what activities as trustees they had engaged in during the previous year and which of these they found difficult. They were also asked to rate their agreement with five statements about their awareness of conflict between trustees and parents or staff, their satisfaction in being trustees of Highland, and their view of their role should Highland become fully funded by tax dollars. Fifteen acting or former trustees responded.

Years of Service and Recruitment

Every trustee had given long service, at least three or four years; six had given "six or more." These years of service represented considerable stability, without which the patient task of generating, developing, and following through on funding contacts could not occur.

Nine of the trustees had been recruited to the group by other trustees, five by staff or parents of Highland, an example of the "each one reach one" approach. The trustees therefore appear to be largely a self-perpetuating group, which is both a strength and a weakness. It is a strength because those already in the group make excellent recruiters; it is a weakness because potential trustees are limited to the pool of people personally known to the current trustees. One trustee respondent wrote of this difficulty: "Fundraising is difficult only because it is not easy to break into the sphere of influential people who control the corporation/foundation gifts."

Activities

When asked to check off the activities they had engaged in during the past year as Highland trustees, all indicated they had done fund-raising and contributed personal funds. All active trustees had attended at least some monthly trustee meetings (only one emeritus trustee had not); all but three active trustees had attended other school functions in the past year, such as graduation; and all but one said they had advised and otherwise supported the parent Board of Directors and staff of the school. A majority had engaged in community relations on behalf of the school. One trustee wrote that she had gotten the annual report brochure designed as a donation and that she herself had edited copy for the report. To be a trustee of Highland Community School, therefore, is to spend your time and energy as well as your money.

Difficulties in Being a Trustee

Asked to check any aspects of being a trustee that were most difficult, eight checked fund-raising, one writing that it was difficult primarily because it was time-consuming. Recalling Frank Miller's comment that "it takes great will" to ask for money, I would suspect that, although no one mentioned it in the survey, just continually asking for money is difficult in itself.

The theme of being busy surfaced only slightly, however. Only one trustee checked "attending trustee meetings" as being difficult, three checked "attending other school functions." One checked "engaging in community relations." These are very busy people, but they did not mind giving their time to Highland. A few regretted only not being able to give more. Being outside the circle of the wealthy and powerful as a difficulty was alluded to earlier, but their working hard and agonizing over their efforts to raise money probably helps Highland's trustees form a bond with those working daily at the school.

Cooperation with Parent Board and Staff

I asked the trustees to rate their agreement with five statements about their relations with parents and staff, their satisfaction with their role, and their understanding of their role in the school. The first statement asked them to rate their awareness of trustee-parent Board conflicts. Virtually every respondent said that they knew of no conflict between the Parent Board and the trustees, although one trustee wrote that he thought there was "some conflict over fundraising and budget issues," without being more specific. There was also strong agreement that there was no conflict between trustees and staff. These trustees' responses corroborate Sally Lewis's comment that the trustees really believe that the parents (and the staff) can run the school.

Trustee Satisfaction

Trustee satisfaction with their role was measured by agreement with two statements. The first asked whether they would sign up for another term after the current one was up. Most indicated that they would do so, although one wrote that "I like Highland, I just feel five years is an appropriate amount of time to serve." The second statement asked whether their work with Highland was one of the more satisfying of their public involvements. The average response was a resounding yes. It is clear from this evidence that the trustees as a group find their involvement with Highland to be very satisfying, which probably accounts for their lengthy service and their willingness to sacrifice their personal resources on Highland's behalf.

Trustee Role

The last item on the survey asked, in effect, whether they saw themselves as merely fund-raisers for the school or whether their role was more complex. It asked whether they saw any role for the trustees at Highland, in the event Highland's entire budget were to be publicly funded. Everyone saw a role for the trustees even if it did not include fund-raising. One wrote, "The role would change but not disappear. They need assistance on budgeting and financial reporting, for example." Another wrote, in effect, that the school would still require access to the expertise of the trustees in handling public funds appropriately. (Highland, however, has received some portion of its budget from public funds almost since its inception. I can think of USDA funds for free and reduced price lunches and day care funds from Milwaukee County in its earliest years, for example.)

Few trustees wrote general comments at the end of the survey, but two did. The first wrote of some frustration at "the time it took to 're-educate' administrators." The second commentator wrote, "The size of Highland and its often precarious budget makes recruitment [to the trustee group] a challenge." Given Highland's "grass-roots" nature, that is, that it is very small and its parent and staff leadership has always been stubbornly self-assertive, trustees used to corporate business culture can occasionally find Highland's brand of democracy a source of mild irritation. These comments simply reveal the different worlds that trustees and Highlanders from the neighborhood inhabit, nothing further. To the contrary, the evidence is overwhelming that, in their own way, Highland's trustees are as committed to the school's purposes and existence as any other group in the school.

Trustees for an Urban Public School?

This commitment to the school's work underlies all else about the trustee group. But it did not spring full blown from the beginning; it was built bit by bit over the years. A leader in an urban public school contemplating the formation of such a group would realize that at first it would probably be a small group of individuals who could function as consultants to the school. In fact, it would probably start as Highland's group did, with the administrator calling on a professional friend for a favor, and proceed from there: "each one reach one."

What would these individuals consult about? First, even though the fund-raising component would be far less, any public school, especially an urban school, has need of further funds for educational materials and activities than are budgeted. The network of public education foundations around the country explicitly acknowledges this need. Such trustees could help raise these precious extra dollars, including contributions from their own pockets. The difference between this arrangement and relying on a public education fund is that the trustees would be raising money for a specific school, and their personal allegiance to, and knowledge of, that particular institution would tend to make them more effective.

Furthermore, the experts from the downtown central office could not take the place of a trustee group. Although the central offices of large public systems usually contain resource individuals, such as curriculum supervisors, research analysts, social work supervisors, and accounting personnel, these people may not only be distant from the school, but because of their evaluative status with regard to each school, there may even be an adversarial relationship. A voluntary group of resource people with allegiance to the target school would probably function more harmoniously with the school. In addition the school may have needs, such as helping staff plan together without conflict, that could not be met by calling on central office personnel.

In the final analysis, Highland's community extends throughout the entire Milwaukee metropolitan area by including the trustees. Highland has found a way to bridge the gulf between economic strata in our cities, by providing meaningful ways to involve the better-off in the lives of the lesser-off. Each urban public school could build a similar bridge. Highland demonstrates that there are many individuals who will walk across it.

The next chapter closes our analysis of Highland's marks of success. It describes the Montessori curriculum as Highland has augmented it.

Chapter Eight
Highland's "Early School" Curriculum

> *To those who say that Montessori is not for every child, I would say that for every child there is something to be learned from Montessori.*
>
> *Elizabeth Hainstock (1986, p. 25)*

Highland's Montessori curriculum spans six years, three years of pre-school and the first three of elementary school. This curriculum functions as a coherent whole which builds and solidifies student understanding of the curriculum content. The first section describes the Montessori model and reviews relevant research on it. Classroom observations and teacher interviews flesh out descriptions of Highland's Children's House (3–6 years) and Junior Level (6–9 years). A following section highlights how Highland has augmented the Montessori model. Finally, Highland's curriculum is compared to contemporary national reform experiments, especially Howard Gardner's "school for understanding" and James Comer's "relationship-building process" in schools.

Understanding the Montessori Model

This section briefly sketches the interaction of the three tripods of the Montessori model: the child, the environment, and the adult. A brief discussion of early criticism of Montessori's pedagogy precedes a short argument that she was actually ahead of her time in understanding the psychology of the young child and developing a pedagogy to match it. Finally the section reviews research on the model.

Montessori Education Model

The term "Montessori" refers to the philosophy and pedagogical practices of Maria Montessori, Italy's first woman physician, who established schools for the children of Rome's slums at the turn of the century. Although her principles and practices quickly gained popularity in Europe, for a variety of reasons they were slow to gain acceptance in the United States. Russia's launching of the Sputnik satellite in 1957 gave impetus to renewed interest in education reform in general and Montessori private schools in particular. And with the advent of the magnet school concept as a viable method of desegration during the 1970s, many public schools took up her methods, joining the already existing network of private and independent schools that have given allegiance to her pedagogy for the past eighty years.

Dr. Montessori's overarching educational goal was to improve the child's quality of life, which implies more than academic learning. The child will achieve a higher quality of life, Montessori thought, to the extent that he or she achieves a sense of autonomy and independence. The need to develop this fundamental sense of self-direction in children therefore underlies all else that Montessori proposes. Her system for doing so could be thought of as *an interactive triangle emphasizing the child, the environment, and the adult.*

The Child

Foreshadowing the developmental psychologists, such as Jean Piaget, Dr. Montessori contended that the child is not simply a small adult, but a unique individual who develops according to hierarchical and sequential stages through the interplay between genetic predisposition and context. Perhaps her most fundamental insight, however, was that the young child possesses an "absorbent mind," that is, a great capacity for learning by observation. "Impressions do not merely enter the child's mind," she wrote, "they form it" (Montessori, 1967, p. 25). The child passes through what she called "sensitive" [critical] periods, during which the child seems instinctively able to choose from the complex environment those activities that are suitable and necessary for his or her growth. She identified sensitive periods for language, movement, and refinement of the senses (throughout preschool); for order (ages 2–4); social skills (ages $2^1/2$–6), and writing (ages $3^1/2$–$4^1/2$) (Turner, 1992).

The Environment

In writing of the child's response to the environment of the school, which she called the "prepared environment," Montessori emphasized the need for it to help focus the child's attention, to create a "society of children," and to facilitate the child's "explosion into writing." The ideal prepared environment itself would be a real house (she called her preschool "the children's house") filled with artistically beautiful materials and child-sized furniture. These materials would elicit from the child a variety of learnings, as opposed to, say, single-answer worksheets:

For example, the concept of length is derived from the red rods of varying lengths. Language is clarified by discussing long and short. Because the rods are rendered in unit lengths from one to ten, they also provide a basis for mathematical gradation. (Kahn, 1992, p. 198)

Although there is a defined set of didactic materials a Montessori-trained teacher employs in her classroom (her "prepared environment"), most teachers add to these materials many others which follow the same principles of aesthetic and multisensory design, developmental appropriateness, and multiple learning possibilities. The following description of the Montessori model at the Junior, or elementary, Level is offered by David Kahn, the executive director of the North American Montessori Teacher's Association:

The [elementary] Montessori classroom offers diversified timelines, picture charts, other visual aids, and practical activities providing a linguistic and visual overview of the first principles of each discipline. Integrating the arts, sciences, geography, history, and languages inspires the imagination of the children. Live specimens heighten the strong orientation toward zoology, botany, anthropology, geology, and the like, exposing children to scientific laws and new vocabulary. Mathematics is presented through concrete materials that simultaneously reveal arithmetic, geometric, and algebraic correlations. The presence of reference books instead of textbooks reflects the emphasis on open-ended research. Finally, learning ventures outside the school are basic to the organization of the classroom. The students themselves organize these outings as a natural extension of their in-school interests. (Kahn, 1992, p. 197)

The Adult

The teacher is the director of the child's *spontaneous* work. At varying stages, the teacher is the keeper of the prepared environment, an entertainer of the children, and optimally the observer and protector of the child's concentration. The Montessori teacher's attitude is even more important than his or her knowledge; the ideal Montessori teacher is self-confident, tolerant, open, and sensitive to others, all prerequisites for being an astute observer and mentor of children.

In summary, the Montessori model assumes that children are natural learners and that the teacher's role is observer and preparer of the environment. Children construct their own knowledge, and the context must support that effort, allowing children choices in what they work on and how long they work. Montessori's approach is holistic: the teacher creates not a mere array of didactic materials but a unique social and psychological milieu that supports the child and the child's developing autonomy and independence. Individual work is of premier importance, but children also learn through social interaction in a multiage grouping.

Though most Montessori programs in the United States are preschools, many hundreds include early elementary (grades 1–3), and there are over fifty programs extending Montessori principles and methods through middle school (grades 7–8). Montessori schools are diverse, however, in terms of their adaptation to local conditions and cultures. And indeed, some schools calling themselves Montessori may be far from qualifying as such.

Early Criticism of Montessori

There have always been critics of Montessori's pedagogy, no doubt spurred in part by the authoritarian ways in which she promulgated her ideas and trained her teachers. In the early years of the century, she was viewed as out of step with pedagogical theory. William Heard Kilpatrick of Columbia University's highly influential Teachers College, for example, pronounced her method to be simplistic and outdated. Although the adoption of her method in this country's public schools was doused by Kilpatrick's wet blanket, it survived in private tuition-supported schools, especially after the Sputnik launching in 1957 heightened criticism of U.S. public education. Since the early 1970s her method has become popular within public systems through the development of magnet schools. As her ideas have become open to wider scrutiny, she has come to be seen as an educator of vision.

Montessori's Emphasis on Early Education Justified

Montessori's understanding of young children's psychology was prescient, as subsequent research has shown. A major area for study has been the transition in the way children think between the ages of five and seven, called the "5- to 7-year shift." Jean Piaget studied the intellectual advances children make during this time and theorized that they were due not to learning but to developmental processes, which are "wired in" and unfold through the child's interaction with her environment. For example, four-year-olds shown a vase filled with white mums and yellow marigolds and asked whether there are more marigolds or more flowers, will usually reply that there are more marigolds than flowers. Seven-year-olds will say that all are flowers, but that only some are marigolds, so that there can't be more marigolds than flowers. Piaget labeled the early stage intuitive or "preoperational," a cognition influenced by appearances. The next stage he termed "concrete operational," wherein the child's logic is grounded in conceptual categories. In a simplistic manner of speaking, the older child was seen as logical and the younger was illogical or "prelogical."

Even the way preschoolers and elementary children think about themselves shows this fundamental distinction between thinking based on appearances and thinking based on developed categories. A preschooler will describe himself by referring to his own behavior: I can jump high, I like pizza. The seven-year-old will use higher-order generalizations to describe herself: I am smart. I am popular. According to Piaget, these shifts result from the reorganization (development) of the individual's cognitive structures; he felt they could not be speeded up by pedagogical means and that the ability to learn formal academic skills must be preceded by certain developmental stages.

Current thinking about the "5- to 7-year shift," however, has moved away from a belief in a cognitive reorganization that later "permits the child to be educated" (Sameroff and McDonough, 1994). Younger children do seem to have the logical precursors which underlie particular behaviors. If the tasks are simplified enough and if motivation is maximized, preschoolers can be taught, for example, to speak in complex sentences, to read, and even to solve mathematical puzzles. Sameroff and McDonough (1994) also indicate that young children whose parents talk to them, asking them what happened when, where, and with whom, have children who have more extensive memories than children whose parents do not talk with them.

Maria Montessori's understanding of the young child's sensitive periods and her notion of the "absorbent mind" foreshadowed these research-based insights into young childrens' cognitive growth. Current thinking about developmental stages has moved away from age-rigidity toward an acknowledgment of *some* age-flexibility under appropriate environmental conditions. Old-fashioned ideas that children cannot be educated until they are seven have crumbled under decades of evidence that the education of young children in formal settings which simplify tasks and maximize motivation merges naturally with movement into elementary school.

An Overview of Research on Montessori Programs

John Chattin-McNichols (1992) reviewed much of the research done on Montessori programs. Most studies he cited have been of preschool programs; less research exists on programs beyond preschool. He categorized studies under two headings. The first he called *process* by which he meant analysis of the types of student-student and teacher-student interactions fostered by the Montessori method as contrasted with other early childhood curriculum models. The second classification of studies concerned *outcomes* of Montessori programs.

Comparisons of the *process* of Montessori classrooms with other preschool models found that role-play was going on at moderate levels and that conversations were occurring at fairly high rates, contrary to claims by critics that the Montessori method allowed no opportunity for fantasy play or socializing among young children. In fact one study revealed that Montessori children spent sizable amounts of time teaching each other.

Comparative *outcomes* of Montessori programs can be clustered into several categories. Though Montessori student gains in general verbal intelligence were slightly less than those for children from some other more directive programs, such as Bereiter-Engelmann, a heavily didactic program with a behavioral orientation (it is the antecedent of the DISTAR program, a behavioral program in wide use today) these gains were more resistant to decline. Researchers (Miller & Dyer, 1975) hypothesized that this effect was due to Montessori's emphasis on concentration and focus in learning. Montessori children gained less on measures of academic achievement and school readiness than children in preschool programs that emphasized direct training in academic areas and language skills. But again, Montessori gains were less likely to fade and did not fade at all if the Montessori experience was continued into elementary school. The Montessori method was also successful in aiding development of visual-motor coordination.

There is evidence that Montessori programs were effective in increasing children's ability to pay prolonged attention to school tasks (Chattin-McNichols, 1992, p. 90). On Piagetian tasks, no programs were able to accelerate movement through cognitive stages, as Piaget would predict they could not, but Montessori seemed more successful than other programs in developing seriation (i.e., ordering according to some scheme such as smaller to larger or shorter to longer) and classification (i.e., categorizing) skills, which are basic to reasoning (Chattin-McNichols, 1992, p. 93). On tests of creativity, results again were mixed. On Torrance tests of creativity, Montessori children did less well than children in traditional nursery school programs, but on tests of divergent verbal production, in which children are asked to tell as many different uses as they can of objects such as a stuffed toy dog, a fork, a Montessori button frame, and a triangular wooden shape, Montessori children outperformed their traditional counterparts (Brophy & Choquette, 1973).

To summarize the outcome research, children in preschool programs focused in one area, such as language skills or perceptual development, outperformed children from Montessori schools in those areas. On the other hand, the Montessori method was superior in helping children to develop attentional strategies, to enhance their seriation and classification skills, and to maintain gains they made in areas of academic achievement (Chattin-McNichols, 1992, p. 96).

The Highland Children's House (Three to Six Years)

The Children's House has three large rooms in a row, connected by sliding double doors, which when opened, give the effect of the three rooms being one room the length of the building. There is a huge foyer to one side of the first two rooms. These four rooms contain two ornate fireplaces, extensive finished woodwork, eleven-foot ceilings, and finished oak floors with parquetry designs. Total floor space is about 1,400 square feet, enough to accommodate forty-five children and four adults comfortably. All the surfaces are hard, but the noise level is pleasantly low, despite movement and children's conversations. There are no curtains on the windows and few items on the walls, although one poster at adult eye-level announces, "It will be a great day when our schools get all the money they need and the Air Force has to hold a bake sale to buy a bomber." Another poster simply states "Africa" in large letters under the profile of an elegant-looking native African woman.

The Children's House space is two similar areas. Tim and his assistant, a mother with children in the school, have charge of two rooms. Maribeth Pinkerton and her assistant, Eniola Oladeji, a school parent for a decade, run the other two. Children may move between them if they wish, but few do. Last year, Tim says, they tried a team approach with all forty-five children and four adults, but abandoned that arrangement this year because, although it worked well for the older children, the youngest ones were "just lost and confused." There are no bells or timed class periods.

Tim's Classroom

It is May, 1991. I am a visitor in the classrooms. Tim walks by holding two children by the hand, all walking deliberately on the balls of their feet trying to minimize noise. The two children now with Tim sit on the floor with him while he brings out a basket with a number of blue wooden geometrical shapes. Two more children spontaneously join them around the small rug on which the basket sits. The other sixteen children in Tim's group are busily engaged in a variety of tasks. Tim rubs his thumbs and fingertips together, asking them to do the same, in order to sensitize them to touch. Then he handles the first wooden shape, a cube, saying "cube." He hands the cube to the girl on his left; she imitates his handling of the cube, but adds holding it to her cheek and on top of her head. "Cube," she says, handing it to the boy on her left. And on around the small circle. Next is "cone," after that, "cylinder," then "ovoid."

Maribeth's Classroom

In both sections of the Children's House, the younger the children, the more they are interested in any visitor who comes into the room. In Maribeth's area, two girls and a boy cluster around me, and Eniola has to take them in hand to help them find things to do. The constant message in this free-movement space is: keep busy. You can do what *you* want to do—at least for a while—but you have to keep busy. It is told often and in many ways. The intent is to promote concentration and discourage the young children's tendencies toward distraction.

In the next room, the Broad Stair and Pink Tower blocks are alternately stacked on a small rug into a free-standing structure the height of a child. No one is near it for the moment, and it is not threatened, even though children walk by it regularly. Eniola is now working on the floor with two boys, building words from cutout red letters. In the other room Maribeth listens to a child read to her at her table. All the other children are engaged in various tasks using materials they have been introduced to previously and which they are learning to master.

Comments and Observations about the Children's House

The teachers' interactions with the children are gentle: no shouting, no putdowns, no sarcasm. Teachers are businesslike but pleasant, soft-voiced but competent and purposeful. The younger children do not interact with each other as much as the older ones do, which is normal for their age and development. But they also do not get in one another's way, and occasionally they chat amiably. Everyone is engaged in work most of the time on this bright warm day in late May.

One of the most noticeable features of a Montessori Children's House classroom is the combination of careful movement and relative quiet among the children. Although they are free to move about at will and to choose work for as long as they may wish, they must respect others' spaces. Each child, upon choosing some materials for work, such as the blue geometric solids mentioned above, sets a small rug in place on the floor and places them on it. That is the child's space, and no one is to invade it. The same goes for table space. Noise levels are kept low by constantly teaching and modeling for children how not to be noisy: the listening game, the teacher's voice level, the practice of deliberately and gently placing objects on surfaces, such as carrying a bell without its ringing and setting it down without banging. Low noise levels foster concentration, one of the hallmarks of the Montessori method.

Another obvious feature the visitor experiences is the array of materials. The rooms are filled with low shelves, themselves stocked, although not crammed, with dozens of objects one is likely never to have seen before. Yes, there are books and reading corners, art corners, possibly play corners for make-believe for the younger children. But many other items are deliberately selected for their use in the children's learning and development that are standard equipment in Montessori classrooms: beads and blocks designed to teach mathematical and geometrical concepts; utensils geared to aid gross and fine motor development in the practical life area, such as sponges and buckets for tablewashing, button and zipper frames, small pitchers for pouring and mixing. The learning of letters and words for reading and writing is facilitated by large sandpaper letter boards, by boxes with compartments for letters of the alphabet, and by a myriad of other materials.

These materials all "fit together." Any Montessori-trained teacher—anyone, for that matter, who has spent several months working in such a classroom even without formal preparation—will recognize them as a coherent whole. In fact, the Montessori classroom, and the entire Montessori school, is a place in which all working there know what all the teachers are doing and why they are doing it. The materials, the seemingly unstructured interactions between teacher and student and among students themselves, the pace, the methods of evaluation, are all of a piece. In the current argot of the business world, everyone is on the same page with regard to both the long-range vision of enhancing the children's quality of life and the day-to-day operations of the school, which promote concentration, independence, and self-confidence.

How do these observations correlate with what research literature on Montessori process and outcomes indicated? First, research suggested that Montessori was superior in helping children develop concentration. Eniola Oladeji, who moved from Children's House Assistant to Junior Level Assistant after several years, spoke about why their concentration develops:

The children can stay with the material they've chosen until their inter-est wanes. Concentration comes from within and flows naturally. The Montessori materials have a built-in control; they're self-correcting (in building the pink tower, for example, a child will see if a block is out of place in sequence without being told), and children will repeat their work with them spontaneously until they've mastered them.

Maribeth Pinkerton, the other Children's House teacher, adds an-other reason why Montessori at Highland helps children concentrate.

Maria Montessori desired that the children's house be called a real house, where children could feel secure enough to concentrate. It's the peaceful, homey atmosphere at Highland that counterbalances the anxiety many of the children experience in their home surroundings. Here, besides us-ing the didactic materials at their own pace, they can talk about their fears and their anger over incidents they might've witnessed at home or in the neighborhood.

Second, research indicates that the didactic materials in the Children's House promote the development of classification and seriation skills. Eniola pointed out that most of the "sensorial" materials, Montessori's term, require that children use their visual and tactile senses in order to grasp the concepts of longer and shorter, larger and smaller, even before words are attached to them. For example, the child lays out the red rods so that the shortest rod is placed first; the next rod, which is twice the length of the first, is laid next to it; the third rod—three times the length of the first—next to the second, and so on through all ten. (This exercise also helps lay the foundation for understanding the base ten and the decimal system, but these are not taught.) Regarding classification, the geometric shapes and sol-ids are examples of the many materials and exercises that help de-velop children's skills in putting things (and ideas) into categories.

The Montessori Model at the Junior Level in Highland Community School

Ideally, a child enters Highland at the age of about three and remains until finishing third grade, or nine years of age. The first two years in the Children's House are half-day programs. Third-year children, the five-year-olds, stay for the "Extended Day" program four days a week. Highland's *Parent Handbook* states, "It [the Extended Day Program] is a time for group activities such as cooking, building, camping, swimming, skating, exploration of the museum, etc. It is a period of preparation and transition from the Children's House to the Junior Level class." The Junior Level is a multiaged grouping analogous to the first three elementary grades, running full days, five days per week, for the six- to nine-year-olds.

Adapting to the Child's Need to "Become a Member of Society"

The rationale for these particular age-groupings is drawn from the views of Maria Montessori but is also rooted in the experience of the teachers. According to Tim Souers, the principal who also teaches in the Children's House in the morning and Extended Day in the afternoon, children up to their sixth year are "focused on themselves." But around five they typically show a need to "see how everything has to fit together," what Montessori called the transition to the "cosmic mind." As Tim put it,

In particular, they are making the transition into the social world. I mean a six-year-old (in terms of cognitive and linguistic development) can do almost everything I can do—and do it with more energy. What they have not learned is how to operate socially. A normal child by six has achieved self-confidence "I can do."; a normal child by nine achieves self-assurance "I am acceptable." But those six- to nine-year-olds are monsters, in a sense. To them fairness is everything; they care if it's fair to them but don't give a damn if it's fair to others. There is a lot of baiting, fighting, and manipulating that goes on at this age, and the curriculum has to be built to help children through that.

Mary Ann Erdtmann, mother of seven children herself, former journalist, and a former public school Montessori Children's House teacher, is the Junior Level teacher who replaced Paige Prillaman in the 1991–92 school year. Mary Ann reinforced the importance of the curriculum's adapting to the great transition that occurs around five to six as the child attempts to become, in her words, a "member of society." "We work in small groups much more than the younger children do in the Children's House downstairs," she said. "Our children need to learn to work together. We emphasize social problem solving as much as possible, and we try to be proactive rather than reactive."

Chapter 2, on cultural diversity, listed five ways by which the Highland Montessori curriculum does this: (1) a few clear, positively stated rules explained at the beginning of the year, with each child signing an "I Care" contract to obey them; (2) the Thursday Class Council at Junior Level to discuss classroom conflicts that arise each week; (3) Tim's "I Care Club," which includes the Extended Day students and uses a formal curriculum to develop alternative ways to solve interpersonal conflicts; (4) the modeling of cooperative relationships by all adults working in the school; and (5) the "superhelper" program, whereby the oldest students can volunteer to mentor younger ones, tutor, or otherwise help out in the school. Although these methods were not originally devised by Maria Montessori, they are compatible with her theoretical emphasis on the child's moving toward the "cosmic mind" or "becoming a member of society."

The Cognitive Curriculum in Highland's Junior Level

In social matters the curriculum at Highland is quintessentially Montessorian in its adaptation to the changing needs of the growing child. In the realm of "content," Mary Ann spoke of "starting with the universe and finding something that they're interested in from the many areas of the curriculum: botany, zoology, history, geography, math, language, art." Attentive to Montessori's emphasis on the "reasoning mind" of the six- to nine-year-old, she introduces each lesson with a story or vignette, such as the ways the Egyptians used to measure length using body parts like arms or legs or feet. The stories get student interest, but they all aim toward cognitive growth, what some educators call "critical thinking." Classification themes run throughout the curriculum:

We classify the kinds of nouns using a story; the zoological classification of animals begins with a story. The commutative and associative laws of math are set within problem stories. Stories from history give insight into the fundamental needs of humans: habitat, sleeping, eating, reproducing, caring for children—just the same categories as the animals.

A third-grader hinted at the use of the story approach when she wrote the following for the spring 1992 edition of the school newsletter:

I like going to Highland because we go swimming. I like the computers we have. I learned how to do division with fractions. This is how you do it. Let's say the problem was 3 divided by 2. We'd get out 3 wholes which we'd pretend are pizzas for two people. . . . Each person would get 1-1/2 pizzas!

In the Montessori model, the transition to what she termed the "cosmic mind," occurring as children enter the Junior Level years, implies that their education will literally take them beyond the classroom walls. "The classroom can't meet all the children's needs for information and understanding," Mary Ann continued, "so we've developed a resource bank of parents to take them on unusual field trips in addition to the regular ones." For example, one parent took three children who expressed interest to a factory that builds railroad trains. A parent who is a nurse took several children on a tour of her work site. Another parent, interested in history, plans to involve many of the Junior Level children in digging into the history of the Highland School building itself—after a cache of old photos, letters, and cards was found behind a mantlepiece in the classroom.

In 1991, I had observed the Junior Level classes. Review of my notes made me realize how Highland's Montessori elements of promoting social growth and cognitive learning had been operating then. All the materials Kahn (1992) had proposed as necessary to the elementary Montessori classroom were present. The children were engaged in using some of them, such as timelines and picture charts. They were also using other materials perhaps particular to Highland. Here is my reconstruction of that visit. On this day (in 1991) the Junior Level (grades 1 through 3) has twenty children; a lead teacher, Paige Prillaman; and her assistant, Brenda deWindt, a parent of three children in the school. The space on the second floor is three large former bedrooms, interconnected in an L-shape. A section of one wall has been removed to enhance adult vision. The windows are seven feet tall and occupy most of one wall in each room, half-curtained in charming fashion. Two of the rooms have ornate fireplaces; the space is carpeted, the ceilings nine-and-a-half feet high.

Shortly after I sit down in a corner opposite Paige's table, where she monitors the assorted work of several children, a student quietly wants to know what I'm doing. I say I'm making some notes on this classroom and ask what he's doing. He is writing down what he's done so far today and what he plans to do. I ask if he'll show it to Paige. "No," he says, "I just keep it for myself." As he walks away, I say thank you. He very carefully responds, "You're welcome." I am reminded of Highland's Montessorian emphasis on social skill building and courtesy.

Paige sits on a child-size chair at a table in the middle room. She can see what's happening in two rooms; Brenda is in the third. Several children in turn come to Paige, most to practice reading from short books, others to show her work they're doing in math or geography (several are coloring maps of continents and their countries). One is making drawings of Ninja Turtle figures, writing captions then pasting them into a booklike arrangement. Several children chat about the upcoming three-day camping trips to Upham Woods in the heart of Wisconsin. One girl, Andrea, has covered her face with red, green, blue, and brown felt tip pen marks. Her lips are apple red. Paige says calmly, "Morning is for working, Andrea. You may go to the bathroom and clean up." Paige then walks around a bit in the other room to monitor the children's work, then tells me, "They're going camping tomorrow; everyone's excited." I had just written in my notes that although there was a lot of movement by the kids, it was controlled. Andrea returns, her face clean but her lips still apple red.

The room Brenda monitors has more furniture than either of the other two, although it is not cluttered. There is a reading loft with soft pillows, under which are three computers on a long table. There are ten children and Brenda. But the noise level is manageable, although Vanilla, the parakeet, chirps loudly in my ear. Five girls coloring their maps together have an extended discussion about how far from their porches their mothers will let them go. Two are not allowed off the porch. The "table" on which they are coloring is the top of a big hamster cage. Two other girls are coloring people figures. One African American girl says to her Caucasian companion, "You colored her black with blond hair; how can that be?" Brenda remarks that one of the girls is too loud. "You don't even realize it," she says again without irritation. Then the fire alarm goes off; the firefighters from the nearby station are here to conduct the monthly fire drill. Everyone leaves quickly and efficiently, and outside, the children behave calmly while they wait for the captain to complete a quick inspection of the building. Their return to the building is orderly as well.

How Highland Extends the Montessori Model

Highland has augmented the Montessori method significantly, even while the school has faithfully implemented it in its fundamentals. According to Tim Souers, a trained Montessori teacher with a master's degree in special education and experience in directing both a public Montessori magnet school and a private, tuition-funded Montessori school in Milwaukee, Highland has added much to the Montessori model in the areas of cultural awareness, music and art, and gross motor development.

Montessori is a closed system. At Highland we haven't modified anything in the areas of practical life, sensorial materials, language, or math. These are all tremendously effective in laying the foundations for later learning. In this regard, the older I get, the more Montessori I get. I've moved away from the open classroom leanings I had in the early 1970s. In the cultural area, however, physical geography is ok, but it's not enough; much, much more is needed in the model. Music and art aren't done as well, either, so Montessori needs to be augmented there. And there's no physical or gross motor in Montessori; but we try to do a lot more there with dance, music, and food [in the multicultural celebrations]. Montessori was naive about the [prepared] environment being enough to change the child. We live in a hostile environment and have to be active change agents. She was not a critical evaluator; she was like a—

what's the word?—a Libertarian; she was just very impractical vis à vis the big system. We have to raise the consciousness of the student about the world, but we [follow Montessori in that we] do it by absorption [rather than by preaching].

One of Tim's final comments on the implementation of the Montessori model at Highland highlights how much importance he places on the values of Highland. "At Highland we would hire a *non*-Montessori teacher with Highland values over a trained Montessori teacher without Highland values."

An example of how Highland augments the Montessori model in music, gross motor development, and cultural awareness occurred when I visited in the 1994–95 school year. A consultant, Cynthia Turner, had been coming to the school weekly to teach the children a vocal approach to music which is Hungarian in origin. The "story-songs" I watched her teach the children were not familiar to me, but her technique engaged the children completely, as they hopped, bobbed, and waved their arms about. Other examples of the extension of the Montessori model are that the Junior Level class puts on several plays each year, most of them of a multicultural nature and some of them written by the children themselves. The Children's House students are always invited to these events.

Two different countries are selected each year for extended study. Dance, music, food, and language from each country are featured throughout the year. Other cultural aspects of those countries are introduced according to the availability of people from those cultures who can visit Highland.

Highland's curriculum is both a faithful implementation of the Montessori method and an extension of it. Yet it retains strong coherence, which seems to lie in the connection between the traditional Montessori curriculum and the ways that Highland extends it. This sense of the unity of the curriculum was driven home to me in a discussion with Tim Souers. Tim pointed out how Montessori's multisensory approach and emphasis on concentration promoted depth understanding in the knowledge disciplines, but he thought the idea of teaching for true understanding could be extended. So when we discussed how children develop language, passing through the stage of rigid adherence to rules ("He goed") to a more complex understanding of exceptions ("He went"), Tim had an insight.

We live in a world of exceptions. Just like learning language is learning its exceptions, learning about our world is learning about exceptions. We create naive models of culture [our own] and the family [nuclear]. So if learning is an aid to life, like Montessori said it is, then children have to be exposed to other ways of life, other models of living, so they can break down those stereotypes."

The original Montessori method attempted to lay a foundation for the child's future life not only in the development of cognitive skills but in the very quality of that life, an independence which is socialized. Ninety years later, Highlanders still work to build that cognitive foundation, but to a degree Montessori never envisioned they do so through developing multicultural awareness as a means to the "quality life."

Highland Compared to Other Current National Reform Experiments

Highland has never been an experiment in any strict sense and has never been supported by research grant funds. But a bit more insight into Highland's curriculum may be gained by comparing it briefly with two contemporary experiments in early school programming, Howard Gardner's Project Spectrum and James Comer's approach, which has been labeled the Comer Process.

Howard Gardner's Project Spectrum

In his book *The Unschooled Mind*, Gardner outlined, designed, and implemented a curriculum to promote "understanding" called Project Spectrum. Originating at Harvard and now adopted in several locations across the country, Project Spectrum builds on Gardner's theories of multiple intelligences, that is, that each person possesses a profile of types of intelligence, such as physical-motor, musical-aesthetic, and social, as well as the more commonly understood logico-mathematical or verbal intelligences. The program also incorporates his ideas of a "children's museum," in which interactive exhibits help children direct their own learning, and "apprenticeships," wherein children help artisans as they create their products or accompany adult workers as they perform their duties.

Most of the curricular elements in Spectrum exist at Highland. The Montessori materials help children direct their own learning. Highland's multicultural units engage the children's "multiple intelligences." Both elements seek to develop the child's understanding as opposed to collecting mere rote answers. Adults from the community act as mentors of a sort, such as a firefighter who not only comes to the children's classrooms but also brings them to visit his fire station only two blocks away. Other adults, usually parents, will take a student or two to do extended research on a problem, such as finding out about the history of Highland's building.

Since there is a large, functioning kitchen on Highland's premises, children have always been involved with cooking, and the cook has cooperated with the teachers in teaching more than recipes: orderly procedures, patience, and a few scientific principles as well. Evaluation takes the form of profiles written by teachers.

Theodore Sizer's well-known approach to redesigning high schools (Sizer, 1992) shares Gardner's emphasis on the cognitive. It also echoes some of Highland's features, even though the age ranges are different. For Sizer, school is about intellect, but the curriculum must be coherent, teaching as "coaching" must take place in small interdisciplinary units, and students must demonstrate their competence by means of "exhibitions" (e.g., portfolios, demonstrations, performances). Sizer's emphases on the school as community, the student demonstrating competency, the curriculum as coherent are features Highland exemplifies. Creating an environment for the "school for understanding" requires a foundation of respectful relationships. For all his emphasis on the cognitive failures of schools, Gardner admits this affective basis:

Individual students have a variety of needs, fears, and aspirations and in a world where many of the traditional supports have weakened, much of the burden for providing support falls on the schools. Only if schools are concerned with civility, with fair treatment of all students from all groups, with feelings, interests, motivations, and values as well as with cognitive goals, can such an environment be constructed and sustained. (Gardner, 1991, p. 243)

Highland's curriculum has deliberately programmed for these affective outcomes.

James Comer's Process of Building Relationships Within School

Comer's model, discussed at length in the literature review on parent involvement in chapter 4, systematically builds adult-adult and adult-child relationships in the school. Comer's is among the most widely published strategies for holistically improving urban schools, although Henry M. Levin's Accelerated Schools Model, implemented in the mid-1980s and currently in 300 schools in 25 states, employs a multiyear process to help staff and parents build relationships in the school, which is similar to Comer's (Brandt, 1992). The emphasis of the Comer model is on the school's becoming a functioning community and that the presence of many adults (one's own parents, other parents, staff) sharing a basic sense of purpose can restore the consistency of social fabric to students' lives that our society has unwittingly removed over the past half-century. Kids would learn how to grow up. Later Comer came to see that the curriculum could deliberately reflect, even enhance, this nurturing community of growth.

Highland's experience has paralleled and even added to the Comer model. The chart below compares features of Highland's program with those of a typical "Comer school." As far as curriculum is concerned, however, there appears to be more emphasis on the cognitive at Highland than in a "Comer school," probably because Highland is a Montessori school, although the Comer school could make this emphasis a part of its program if the staff and parents so desired. The Comer model is more formally than Highland a relationship-building approach. Both types of school, however, are strongly oriented toward the affective curriculum.

Highland's curriculum is coherent and unified because it meets the changing needs of its children in all aspects of their development. Its Montessori foundations ground the children in all the skills necessary for academic achievement, especially the ability to apply oneself fully to work without distraction. The curriculum in the first three years conforms to the child's need for individual mastery and competency, then augments that continued need for compe-

Table 8.1 Comer Process and Highland Compared

	Comer School	Highland School
School setting	Low-income urban neighborhood	Low-income urban neighborhood
School type	Public elementary	Independent (nonpublic)
Admission policy	Open within neighborhood boundaries	Open within neighborhood boundaries; parents must agree to participation requirement; racial/ethnic balance sought
Governance	School Planning and Management team; Student Support Services Team; Principal in charge	Elected nine-member board; master teacher as principal; administrator as plant and funding chief
Outside support	Third-party mental health consultants; school district; others possible	Advisory group of trustees as fund-raisers; other community resource people and groups
Organizers on staff	School social worker as main parent organizer	Special parent coordinator, part-time
Parent involvement	All levels, incl. classroom teaching and governance	Required at all levels
Curriculum	Traditional, but includes "social skills" activities and artistic expression	Montessori. Rests on "empowering the child" and helping child to build self-confidence and control
Explicit values	Building community collaboration; modeling social skills	Cross-cultural awareness; building community; nonviolence; valuing children; informal helping network; egalitarianism
Structure	Traditional: K–6	"Early school": three years each preschool and early elementary

tence with an emphasis on social competence. Building on Montessori practices and philosophy, the curriculum at Highland seeks to present the world in all its varieties and differences to counter the most destructive of all naive theories—that the way I am, the way I live, the culture I represent is the world the way it should be.

Summary

This chapter began with an overview of the Montessori model and results of studies done to compare it with other early childhood education models. Montessori, with its emphasis on the spontaneous activity of the child, attention to the child's absorbent mind, and teacher-as-guide, has shown superiority in helping children develop (a) resistance to distraction in academic work and (b) cognitive skills in seriation and classification, the foundations of reasoning.

The chapter depicted the Children's House program for three- to six-year-olds, then the Junior Level for those six to nine years old. Observations and interviews with the teachers at those levels fleshed out how at Highland the cognitive and affective aspects of the curriculum interweave to form a coherent whole. The Children's House focuses on the child's need to become individually competent, though daily the childen are taught how to interact with each other politely and considerately. The Extended Day program for the five-year-olds places yet more emphasis on doing things together cooperatively, and these children are included in the Junior Level's "I Care" program, which discusses peaceful solutions to interpersonal and social conflicts.

The Junior Level blends the children's growing cognitive needs with their becoming, in one teacher's words, "members of society." Academic skills are built more through small group work and cooperative problem solving than occur at the Children's House level because that is more appropriate for these older children. The Montessori structure is just as present in the Junior Level as it is in the Children's House, in the sense that as children gain mastery of a concept they move on to more complex tasks. Academic progress is still measured by mastery of these tasks in order. Highland has augmented the Montessori method's shortcomings in music, art, drama, and gross motor activities by means of its comprehensive approach to multicultural education.

Finally, the chapter briefly compared Highland's curriculum with nationally recognized reform experiments, particularly those of Howard Gardner's Project Spectrum and James Comer. Highland's curriculum parallels Gardner's cognitive emphasis in Project Spectrum. That is, it seeks in a variety of ways to help each child develop understanding as opposed to collecting correct (rote) answers. Highland has programmed heavily for affective learning as well, especially through its multicultural curriculum. In this latter regard for social learning, Highland's emphasis on building relationships in the school among students and among adults and between students and adults resembles the Comer school process.

Chapter Nine
Highland's Lessons for Public Education

The renewal of public education in this country requires nothing less than a frontal assault on every aspect of schooling. . . . Trying to get more learning out of the present system is like trying to get the Pony Express to compete with the telegraph by breeding faster ponies.

Edward B. Fiske (1991), pp. 14–15

What does the Highland experience have to say to those interested in improving urban public schools? Let us briefly review the characteristics of Highland's success before applying these ideas to public education. It is not the intent of this book to script a detailed scenario for change but to suggest what its components might be by describing Highland Community School and to urge public school districts to consider and then act upon these recommendations.

Mission and Values

The sense of mission which has perdured through the years at Highland drives its organizational arrangements and interactions. The people of Highland have striven to provide a quality Montessori education and a nurturing environment for the diverse families from the West Side who have become its members. These families in turn have become "the people of Highland" for those who would follow them, encouraging deep involvement with their children and promoting positive change in their urban surroundings. The values paramount at Highland are respect for all children and families in the culturally diverse neighborhood, a sense of community responsibility anchored in egalitarianism, the nurturance of children, and nonviolence, and the empowerment of all participants in the school, especially parents and children.

The Value of Cultural Diversity

Highland places great weight on attracting and holding a balance of culturally and economically diverse families from the neighborhood. The school's admissions policies give the strongest evidence of this collective intent. And in celebrating the diverse community in their midst, they celebrate that of America itself. Teachers are aware, however, of minority cultures' histories of oppression and plan all multicultural activities with these facts in mind.

The Value of Community Responsibility

Highland makes great demands on all who join. Community at Highland results from the intense participation of all its members and from the overt practice of three other interconnected values. The first is egalitarianism, which blurs roles and avoids at all costs a sense of superiority and inferiority in working relationships. The second value places nurturance of children as the top priority. The third is nonviolence, which counters the violence of the neighborhood by seeking to make relationships between adults and children more positive and less punishing for the children. There are no oaths required for allegiance to these values, but it would be difficult for parents to participate for long in the school without adhering to them to a significant degree.

Autonomy and Local Control

The entire school embodies the value of autonomy. The Montessori pedagogy places special emphasis on developing the young child's sense of independence as the doorway to a high quality of life. Teachers therefore avoid interfering with children's spontaneous interests, acting primarily as guides and designers of the prepared environment. The planning by staff is cooperative, teachers respecting each other's expertise. The administrative functions are also performed in consultation with everyone affected. The parent Board of Directors respects the teachers' autonomy. The trustees and the staff respect the parents' governing capabilities. And although Highland is connected to many funding sources and regulatory agencies, it has final say over its programs and policies.

The pervasiveness of the respect for each participant's initiative and responsibility implies that all who wield the oars on the ship of Highland do so voluntarily. Any true school reform experiment should have such autonomy as its goal (the current jargon phrase is "empowerment"). Without that element, reform will remain superficial.

Organizational Practices

The organizational variables, those aspects of the school subject to programming and policy, flow from the mission and reinforce it. New arrivals, who may not yet understand the mission, see its workings as they are drawn into the programs and live according to the policies of the school. Since this continuous "inclusion" is primarily a parent-oriented process, this section begins with Highland's parent policies and programs, followed by other "organizational inputs": trustees, the curriculum, organization of staff, and some characteristics that are peculiar to Highland but which hold implications for change in public education.

"Parent-Centeredness" of the School

Highland Community School not only allows parent participation at all levels of the school, it demands it. The parents themselves govern the school, and employ a Parent Coordinator to monitor each parent's involvement. Typically, half or more of the staff at any given time are parents whose children attend Highland or have attended the school. There is a close working relationship between parents and teachers, and parent governance of the school paradoxically has allowed professional autonomy for those in the classrooms.

Such demands for parent involvement have been necessary for the school's survival, but the parents themselves gain a great deal from their efforts in the school. This parental participation educates parents in their parent role, providing insights, modeling, and support for childrearing practice which help them nurture their children despite larger environmental and cultural forces which militate against the nurturance of children.

Trustees

Highland's trustee group historically grew from a few professionals who offered the school their legal, financial, and fund-raising services to a more formal group which meets regularly and has charged itself with a major share of the school's fund-raising efforts. After twenty-five years the trustees have become an essential element of the school, connecting it in vital ways to the larger Milwaukee community. The trustees, although they provide advice when asked, remarkably do not interfere in the parents' governance of the school. This confidence which the trustees show in the parents is a unique example of autonomy within the school.

The Montessori Curriculum in an Early School Format

Highland's six-year curriculum, spanning the preschool, kindergarten, and early elementary grades from ages three to nine, forms what I have called an "Early School." The Montessori method grounds students in the fundamentals of language, reading and writing, and mathematics, by using a broad spectrum of carefully designed hands-on materials. Research indicates the method is especially helpful to students in developing their ability to concentrate and enhancing their skills in seriation and classification, necessary for the conceptual tasks of the elementary school.

The Early School combines the advantages of preschool education, the extended day (kindergarten) for five-year-olds, and the first three years of elementary school in a single program. It is the bridge across the gap so decried by researchers who find educationally disadvantaged children losing gains they made in preschool programs after they enter traditional elementary programs. The Early School is the needed step beyond Head Start and Follow Through. Its curriculum is coherently constructed to maximize motivation and opportunities for academic achievement, and to promote socialization to the group while building a sense of independence in each individual student. The Montessori method lends itself readily to this six-year sequence, although Highland has added to the Montessori base extensive offerings in multicultural education, using music, dance, and food activities to engage the whole child.

Another factor in this curriculum, sometimes overlooked, is its multiage grouping. This feature allows discrete groups of students and teachers to stay together for up to three years. Research has discovered that such school groups themselves can be a powerful force for learning, since continuity, persistence, and intimacy are the characteristics of groups highly influential on their members (Wynne and Walberg, 1994).

Staff Organization into a Planning Team

Highland's principal is a practicing teacher. Tim Souers teaches one Children's House morning session each day and takes on the Extended Day children four afternoons a week. But he calls faculty meetings—which include the assistant teachers—sets the agenda for the meeting and functions as mediator if disputes arise between parents and teachers. He also acts as liaison between the parent Board of Directors and the faculty.

Teachers plan together weekly throughout the year and meet informally in subgroups more frequently than that. These meetings insure that each teacher is aware of the others' practice, so that their efforts complement one another. The whole faculty participates in professional development workshops as they can and as the school can afford, but their in-house interactions with each other are a primary learning source for their practice.

Some of Highland's key features are accidents of its context. Its small school population is limited by the size of the building it occupies. Its independent status leaves it always vulnerable to lack of funds. Its presence in a depressed neighborhood requires that its leaders collaborate with other helping agencies and organizations in the area to cope with the problems some of its families bring. Nonetheless, public schools can learn from Highland's response to its environment.

Small Size and Aesthetic Building

Highland's size and its location in a comfortable and aesthetically beautiful large home are important to its success. The building complements the Montessori curriculum, meeting Montessori's standard for an appropriate Children's House setting.

As for size, a study of small rural schools in the Midwest and West in 1994 ("Study") suggests that their higher student test scores were due to their small *school* (vs. classroom) size rather than to their cultural homogeneity. Schools with fewer than 300 students had the highest performances. What all these small schools had in common was (1) a belief that all students could learn shown by their academically challenging curricula, (2) a high degree of local control, and (3) a high degree of parental involvement. In smaller schools, the principals knew every student, and each student stood a far better chance of participating in a variety of school and extracurricular activities.

Highland's small size has been criticized by a few parents, staff, and trustees as *too* small, and suggestions have been made that an optimum size would be around 150, say three or four Children's House groups supporting two or three Junior Level classes. The size of the student body has historically been determined by the building itself, of course. But this criticism is speculative; the evidence presented in this book shows that the current size is successful.

An Independent School

As an independent school, Highland is a "hungry" school. Chronically underfunded, accustomed to watching every precious penny, it hungers for resources. It *needs* the parents of its students, other members of the neighborhood, the trustees who connect it so successfully to the resources of the larger community. It needs these resources absolutely—without them it will quickly expire. Consequently, the school sees in every person connected with it a potential resource, even those adults who start out clientlike and withdrawn. It says to all these people, in many ways, you have to help pull the wagon; no one just rides.

Collaboration with Community Agencies

Despite severe resource constraints, Highland takes seriously the need to reach out to its disadvantaged families by referrals for specific services. There is, however, no formal team of representatives from agencies meeting regularly to discuss, prescribe, and monitor services for these families. Most activity is by informal networking with such agencies as Family/Youth Services, Neighborhood House, and the Women's Domestic Crisis Center.

The limits of this form of Highland's involvement with the community are consistent with research findings. Kathleen Cotton (1991) reviewed the literature on school-community collaborative efforts. If the main problem is coordination of services for disadvantaged families, she concluded, the school can't be the coordinator in most cases. School staff have neither the time nor the professional expertise for such an organizational role. There may be ad hoc case-management teams, however, led by a school principal or teacher which would include representatives from other agencies. A formal collaborative effort of Highland, in which the principal or teacher heads up a team of agency representatives who meet on a regular basis, is probably not feasible in most cases without additional funding. I alluded to these teams earlier, in discussing applications of the Comer model. Individual staff or parents at Highland help each other in times of crisis, as indeed occurs at many other schools. The considerable extent to which it occurs at Highland is an indicator of the commununal cohesiveness which exists there.

A Summary Note on Effectiveness Variables at Highland

The introduction listed a number of factors found in effective schools. This book has shown that Highland exhibits these factors, although there are a few differences, such as trustees substituting for district support and Highland's policy that "homework" is largely confined to school hours until the third year of Junior Level.

Although, according to the research on what makes schools effective, there is a conceptual distinction between organizational variables and values, at Highland there is not a real distinction. The values that drove the creation of the school and maintain it to this day shape Highland's specific policies and activities. In turn, the behaviors of Highland's "old hands" provide models for new parents and staff, reinforcing those values and encouraging rededication to them. There is a circularity to attitudes and behaviors in the successful school. Vision drives action; action refines vision.

What Can Highland School Tell the Public School?

We are now in a position to speak directly to the Milwaukee Public Schools' Superintendent, Dr. Howard Fuller, who asked Highland parents and staff in 1991, "What lessons can we public school people learn from you?" The remainder of the chapter is a detailed response, based on an analysis of Highland's strengths. Although this response is divided into several sections, if anything should be clear from this study, it is that all the factors considered important to school effectiveness are interrelated and interdependent.

Pay Primary Attention to Explicating and Then Living Out the Values of the Reform Mission

Highland's mission statement concisely tells the world that the school values nurturance of children and families, that it embraces the cultural and economic diversity of the neighborhood and uses it to teach. It implies its main curricular values by the one word, Montessori. The school states that it seeks to be a force for change not only in education but also in societal arenas beyond education. Highland is an independent school; its autonomy has enabled it to become a community of nonviolence and nurturance of its members. Its value of egalitarianism has helped to fill in the moats which separate parents and teachers in too many other schools.

Public schools can take on value orientations like these. Shanker (1994b) cited a survey of Americans which indicated there is substantial agreement on what values should be taught in public schools. For example, 95 percent of Americans said that schools should teach respect for others regardless of their racial or ethnic background. And 76 percent said that students should be taught about the struggle for black civil rights in the 1950s and 1960s. In other words, most Americans believe the job of schools includes teaching the values that allow a diverse society to live together peacefully.

Highland, however, has not only taken on and proclaimed its values, it has struggled over the years to embody them. Any reform effort in a school must recognize that it is one thing to agree on a mission statement and quite another to live it out.

Stress Parent Involvement at All Levels in the School

Parent involvement extends to putting parents in key decision-making roles. As multiple experiments by urban districts have shown, however, it is not enough to simply announce that intent or to suddenly start making demands on parents without having built the necessary networks that will draw them in and hold them to the school. James Comer began with grant money to pay parents to be classroom aides in the two inner-city New Haven schools he started working with in 1968. But only after several years were the parent networks established and the suspicions and mistrust on both sides replaced by cooperative work groups composed of both parents and teachers. Highland makes demands of parents' time and resources in return for their children's participation in the school. If any school wants to make big demands on parents, it had better show them a big payoff. The best payoff, of course, occurs as parents see their children profiting by an excellent school program.

Making parents true partners in the school enterprise has two major benefits. First, they can help the school in many ways; they are a tremendous resource; of course, it must always be remembered that this resource has to be cultivated; it has to be planned for, sweated over, and patiently developed. Second, they can learn to be better parents as they work for their children by helping the school. This is what Highlanders mean by saying they "get to the children through the parents."

Start parent involvement by encouraging parent leaders. Parent leadership is the leading edge of parent involvement. Without it, whatever else the inputs, there will be little improvement for children, whether academic or social. A study of how different neighborhood residents interacted with schools (Summerfield, 1971) backs Highland's experience. In a poor, predominantly black, big-city neighborhood, an elementary school principal was immensely successful in attracting physical resources to his school. He got a new, air-conditioned building and a disproportionately high share of federal funds. His school incorporated a neighborhood center under its roof, which provided a range of social services to the school's parents and children. His teacher-pupil ratio was a low 1 to 23, teacher morale was high, and teacher turnover was low. The principal encouraged every curricular innovation he could. Yet underachievement proved intractable, children continuing to score, on average, about two years below norms on all standardized tests.

Parent involvement at this school was nonexistent. Half a dozen parents were a big turnout for an all-school PTA meeting. Yet surveys indicated that most parents quietly supported this principal's dynamic leadership, which consisted of his constant contact with the leaders of 95 agencies and organizations in the neighborhood, and his hugely successful lobbying for resources from the central office. Here was a case where "they fixed the school but it still didn't work." Parent involvement, built on a foundation of parent leadership, is the key to improving schools for children.

Are there parent leaders in poor neighborhoods? Simply, yes. School people wishing to involve parents from low-income neighborhoods should expect to find militants, radicals, and establishment-oriented leaders in their parent bodies, as Curt Lamb (1975) predicts. To be sure, there will be parents, especially young, single mothers, who feel isolated and unable to cope. But as Highland has demonstrated, some of these parents are capable of considerable leadership under the right organizational conditions. Some parents will be alienated and mistrustful, and the school may be one of those institutions they are alienated from. Winning them over is crucial; it begins with the personal concern virtually all parents share for their children's well-being. Other poor parents will come to the school as already successful parents, however. Upon these rocks will be built the parent involvement community. As did Head Start on a larger scale, Highland has demonstrated that many poverty-level parents, given supportive channels to lead or contribute, will do so.

Involve Parents and Other Residents by Asking the Community

Urban schools need help, but they *must* reach out to their neighborhood. School leaders contemplating change will find themselves hungry for people to help them; the neighborhood is where these leaders will begin finding helpers. School leaders must understand that getting parents to help means making them real partners in the school enterprise. Making parents responsible for the school means sharing control of the school with them.

Inner-city public school staff rarely live in their school's neighborhood. Consequently, they tend to fear the area excessively and avoid it. Yet, in even the most apparently God-forsaken stretches, there are always many responsive and responsible people in thriving legitimate businesses, churches, and service agencies. Perhaps the most valuable resource the school can gain in the beginning of any organizing effort is a realistic introduction to the people of the area who can be sworn in to help improve the school.

One of the best places to begin building linkages between school and community is the local neighborhood organization (Williams, 1985, 1989), even though there may not be many parents active as members. Throughout its history, Highland has drawn some of its parent leadership from neighborhood organizations. But even if the public school does not immediately attract such parents, leaders in the neighborhood organization can give good feedback, however, on the realities of the neighborhood, on other key people to contact, and on parent involvement strategies school personnel might be contemplating.

Sometimes there is no neighborhood organization as such; but a church, a tenants' organization, housing cooperative, or community center may perform the same functions of providing a realistic window on the community and its human resources, having established communication networks and performed credible services for people there.

Block clubs, if they exist, may also be sources of parent leadership for the school or of good information about the resources of the neighborhood. They are smaller organizations with few resources, but they may be useful in spite of their limited scope. They are usually social in nature, one step up from chatting across the back fence. If they address any issues, the residents' attitudes are typically characterized by feelings of very high threat to their neighborhood (Hojnacki, 1979), although they usually feel safer on their immediate block.

If no community organization exists in the school's district, the school itself might become a focal point for organizing. Although the "community school" idea, that is, that the neighborhood school be a focal point of extracurricular educational and recreational activity, is nearly a century old, it has never been widely implemented. And it is unlikely that school personnel could start a traditional neighborhood organization or even a block club.

The school itself, therefore, represents a great resource to be shared, even in the poorest neighborhood. First, it can potentially provide, if it is not doing so now, a good education to the neighborhood children. Residents know when the education is good and become fiercely loyal to a local school that they perceive is performing well. On the other hand, too many urban schools are not doing well, leading to widespread resentment on the part of parents and neighbors.

Second, the school can be a community center with meeting rooms, food preparation areas, and indoor and outdoor recreation facilities. The school, therefore, can do many things for the neighborhood besides educating its children, under the right circumstances. A neighborhood service center could be appended to a school, which would make it into a community center, several of which have been developed in Grand Rapids, Michigan (Vann, 1992).

Third, even the typical run-down inner-city "blackboard jungle" elementary school costs about a million dollars a year to operate. There are professional and nonprofessional salaries and a host of other expenses. Neighborhood people could be employed there; contracts for services (painting, snow shoveling, food preparation) could be let to neighborhood businesses. The school is not only neighborhood educator and center, it is potentially a neighborhood employer as well. In short, the school itself can function as a sort of community organization whose focus is educational service.

An overriding goal of restructuring the school should be getting the parents invested in it. But organizing parents is not simply getting them to do what the school wants them to do; it also means making parents partners in the enterprise, being open to doing what they want the school to do. The school shows this openness by sharing its resources with the parents and neighborhood: jobs, contracts, facilities, even its professional expertise.

There is a paradox in creating links between the school and its community. On the one hand, school personnel may perceive that in reaching out to the neighborhood they are being asked to do too much, to go beyond the job descriptions they have become accustomed to. On the other hand, to the extent that they do forge these linkages, they will receive support from those they bring into the school as partners, and their work in the long run will become easier and more fruitful. Modern managers know they must continually reinvest in their operations. In the case of the neighborhood school, investment of personnel time in involving parents and community residents in the school will pay off in program success down the line.

Provide District Support *and* Additional Private Support

Highland's trustees have to do double duty for the school, since it has no district support. (Milwaukee's Parental Choice Program, mentioned in chapter 2, is a state-funded program.) But even public schools are rarely flush, especially in the inner city.

Major contributions since 1993 to an inner-city elementary school in the Grand Rapids Public School system have enabled the school to conduct an experiment which will, after three years, compare its student achievement scores with those of children from a school in an affluent suburb. The hypothesis is that by equalizing school expenditures, in this case to hire extra personnel, children in poverty can achieve educationally as well as their suburban counterparts. Whatever concerns an observer might have about the validity of this idea, and whatever the outcome will be, the fact remains that about 25 percent of the extra funds of $600,000 came from an anonymous contributor in the private sector (Benson, 1994). The "discovery" that this inner-city school had no library to speak of elicited another private contribution of $25,000 to buy books.

Any public school, especially with the help of its district, can begin the slow but important process of building connections to the larger business and professional community, creating its own trustee group, as it were. The key lies in developing personal relationships between potential trustees and school staff, parents, and children. Typical school-business partnerships run the risk of being impersonal, superficial, or short term. The main purpose of such a group as Highland's trustees represent is not primarily fund-raising, however, but *advocacy* for the school. Fund-raising is a main task, however, and follows from the advocacy role.

Make the School Environment Aesthetically Pleasing

Schools can be secure and pleasant in appearance. Too often inner-city schools resemble fortresses or prisons. Highland does lock its doors during school hours, but someone is always there to answer the doorbell promptly. The school is kept clean and is well maintained, and its mansionly features are prized and cared for. Even the plywood radiator covers are artistically sawn and stained. The children's work is displayed attractively alongside other more mature works of art. All the rooms are organized aesthetically, despite plentiful materials for all aspects of the curriculum.

Organize Large Schools into Small Multiage Units

Although Highland was never the result of such a reorganization, it does exemplify the power of the small, multiage unit to educate. According to Diana Oxley (1994), a researcher at Temple University who studies urban schools, breaking schools into small units, or subschools, creates a context for teaching and learning that is more stable, more intimate, and more supportive for teachers and students than large, amorphous groups.

Oxley studied two high schools, one in Philadelphia and one in Germany, that placed students in units of 225 to 250. Each unit consisted of students in several grade levels and of many degrees of ability. Students in these smaller units within the school showed much lower dropout rates than than their peers not in these programs. This kind of radical reorganization of the student population, however, requires significant change of the teachers and in the curriculum.

Organize Teachers into Teams to Plan the Curriculum

Within each grouping in the schools, there should be a team of three or four teachers that plans the year's events and decides who will be responsible for each part of the curriculum. Planning sessions must occur frequently, regularly, and continually throughout the school year. Although experimental schools have given teachers release time to plan together, Highland has never had that luxury. There teachers spend several days before the school year discussing their plans with each other and during the year meet during weekly sessions at the noon hour to plan. Since all the lead teachers are trained in Montessori pedagogy and the Montessori method is a structured educational "package," Highland's teachers have an advantage over non-Montessori teachers. Nonetheless their assistants must be included in the planning, and as we have seen, not all Montessori teachers share exactly the same practices. In answer to those who think no teacher would take extra time to do such planning, it is likely that most teachers who see the opportunity to exercise significant professional autonomy will sacrifice to do so. The following suggestion is a corollary of the team planning concept.

Place Instructional Leadership in the Hands of Practicing Teachers

Highland's principal is simultaneously a practicing teacher. When he went on a year's sabbatical from the principalship although he remained as a teacher, he was replaced by another practicing teacher. The principal chairs the planning sessions, helps the other teachers interact with parents and students, introduces new ideas into the curriculum, and helps teachers and assistants with inservice training. The other administrative staff at Highland, however, concern themselves strictly with organizational maintenance and support of the faculty, but the principal position bridges the administration-faculty gap. In this capacity, the principal is truly an advocate for the teachers, and as one of them he is in a position to know the strengths and needs of each colleague.

This shifting of leadership to within the faculty itself suggests a ranking system similar to the professoriate. Why not have two or three successive ranks that teachers could strive for and achieve with the vote of their peers? If teaching is viewed as a "horizontal" career with little upward professional mobility, the introduction of ranks might speed reform as well as retain excellent teachers as teachers. Current reform discussion focuses far too much on weeding out deadwood and far too little on promoting and reinforcing excellence. At Highland there appear to be three functioning ranks already: the assistant teachers, the lead teachers, and the principal, who acts as a "master" teacher without the negative connotations such a term might carry in an egalitarian environment such as Highland's.

Individualize the Curriculum

From a Montessorian's perspective, this means that the teachers "structure the environment" of the classroom to be educative. All the materials are created so that when children choose to work with them, the materials themselves teach them with minimal teacher intervention. In practice, however, the teacher introduces each new material in a small group setting as the most efficient way to help each child to begin. The rule is that children can use anything in the classroom they've been introduced to, although it takes a while for very young children to become accustomed to this idea. As they gain facility in working on their own, the teacher functions more and more as a guide or consultant, occasionally intervening for a group lesson.

Thus individualization means ultimately that children not only proceed at their own pace, but also choose their own work within the overall structure of the curriculum. The teachers determine the goals and objectives of the curriculum, but the children can participate on a daily basis in deciding what they study. Teachers monitor children's progress in all the areas of the curriculum, however, and urge children to work in areas they seem to be neglecting.

Make the Curriculum Coherent Across Grades

There is much talk about high expectations for students in education. But too many educators translate this into making a curriculum that daunts even the quickest of the students, and too often the pieces of these curricula don't fit together. Lloyd Duck (1981) speaks of this tendency of teachers to take content off in all directions as an "amorphous" view of subject matter. This tendency becomes pronounced when teachers "teach to tests," especially national or district achievement tests.

The curricular optimum would be subject matter that builds on earlier learnings, relates to student experiences, challenges present student knowledge in such a way that with guidance children can learn, and is interconnected as much as possible with other content disciplines. Highland's Montessori curriculum, augmented as it has been, is coherent in this manner. Content disciplines (e.g., math, science, literature) build on materials from previous years. As we saw, teachers show how the disciplines interrelate whenever the opportunity arises. The materials are age-appropriate, and the individualization of the entire program enables teachers to monitor each child's progress, insuring flexibility in challenging each student. Since the school is neighborhood-based and uses the diversity of the student population as a teaching tool, students' experiences of difference and similarity are key ingredients in Highland's curriculum. Highland's many and varied field trips extend children's experiences, especially those of low income who rarely leave their neighborhood.

Provide Teaching Staff with Professional Development Opportunities, Especially Those Supporting Reform

Traditional teachers wishing to change to an individualized teaching approach will require a great deal of inservice training, practice, and support. Highland has little money to send people to conferences, but teachers may attend training sessions run by the public schools or Montessori associations in the area. Several of the school's former teachers have become Montessori teacher trainers and occasionally lend their expertise to current teachers at Highland or the Milwaukee public Montessori schools. The lack of funds for materials and other resources has been a burr under the saddle of Highland teachers for years, however, and on one occasion, at least, caused tensions between some staff and the parent Board of Directors.

Teach Social Skills to Students, Parents, and Teachers

Successful school programs work consciously at helping adults interact cooperatively with each other and students; these programs also teach students explicit skills in resolving conflicts without resorting to violence. Highland's message, from the time of Admissions Committee interview forward, is that Highland demands the cooperation of all who would benefit from its services. Nonetheless, there are specific workshops and programs designed to help parents understand how to interact more positively with their children.

Anyone experienced in school practice, however, knows that the adults in the school need to learn to work together. Successful schools do not leave this to chance but program for it. In one recent dispute that arose at Highland between the teachers and the parent Board of Directors, an outside facilitator was hired to help the opposing sides talk to one another and reach a level of consensus, which they did. Cooperation at Highland is of paramount concern, and when tensions arise, the social machinery has been forged over long years to resolve them.

Develop an "Early School" Approach

Kindergarten (for the year from ages five to six) is an already accepted preliminary to elementary school. Head Start (for the year between four and five) reaches hundreds of thousands of low-income preschoolers. The Early School, a coherent curricular package which would encompass a six-year span—from ages three and six, and then extended through the first three grades—is the next logical step in the public's acceptance of the need for early childhood education, particularly for educationally disadvantaged children.

Highland presents a model for the Early School as an alternative to current compensatory education program. Perhaps grants would support such experimentation in districts bold enough to try it. Perhaps educators could cobble together a program incorporating Head Start and kindergarten, while adding an additional year at the front end, although this latter strategy will be made quite difficult by the existence of already functioning independent programs. The best possibility might be to redirect compensatory education funds into building the Early School program.

Redirect Compensatory Education Funds into Creating an Early School Program

Compensatory education, one legacy of Lyndon Johnson's War on Poverty, enacted in 1965, seeks to "compensate" for the perceived educational deficits of certain low-income children. These children carry the label "educationally disadvantaged."

The Educationally Disadvantaged

Children who are poor, whose parents are uneducated, whose first language is other than English, who are minority, or are cared for by only one parent tend to be educationally disadvantaged. But the term also includes the emerging understanding of education as a process that takes place both inside and outside of schools (Cremin, 1988). That is, educational experiences come not only from the *school* itself, but also from the *family* and the *community*. A child who is educationally disadvantaged has been exposed to insufficient educational experiences in at least one of these three domains.

One implication of this view is that a family may be *socially* competent in rearing a child but not *educationally* competent. The family may be cohesive and loving, yet still not reinforce the child's school experiences. This definition also acknowledges that disadvantage may continue throughout a child's school life even if a particular school is able to meet that student's needs. And finally, the definition allows for variation in the disadvantaged population, for example, a child's needs may be met by the family, but because of the inflexibility of the school in adapting to her learning disability, she is still at a disadvantage educationally.

Earlier we saw that reviews of research on Head Start, kindergarten, and other early childhood programs for educationally disadvantaged children, showed that when the children in the programs entered traditional public schools in the first grade, the academic gains they made typically faded out by the end of third grade (Natriello et al., 1990). Explanations for this fadeout usually focused on elementary teachers' lack of reinforcement of learnings gained in the early childhood program. Consequently a number of reinforcement strategies at the elementary level, under the umbrella of compensatory education, have been tried by the federal government, funded under Title I/Chapter I of the Educational Consolidation and Improvement Act (ECIA) of 1981. About six billion dollars per year go to school districts to fund a variety of programs designed to "compensate" for these educational deficiencies.

"Pullout" Programs

As the population of educationally disadvantaged (ED) students has increased, with its attendant increase in diversity of needs, recent reform movements in the schools of America have tried, in the main, to force this population to adjust to the schools, rather than to adapt the schools to their population's needs. The vast majority of compensatory education programs to meet the needs of ED students are either of the "add-on" or "pullout" variety, add-on including Head Start and summer school programs, pullout referring to the principal remediation activities in elementary schools. In the pullout strategy, children identified as meeting the criteria of educational disadvantage are pulled out of their regular classrooms, either individually or in small groups of three to eight, to be given remedial instruction by specialized teachers.

A few types of compensatory education programs try to "reinvent" the school to make it more flexible: *In-class* programs deliver services to ED students in their regular classrooms. *Replacement* programs provide ED students *all* of the instruction they receive in a given subject, typically in a separate classroom with only other ED students. *Schoolwide* programs deliver services to all students in a school serving an attendance area where at least 75 percent of the students are from low-income families. But for the most part the traditional school structure remains the norm: self-contained classrooms at the elementary level and departmental classes at the middle and high school levels.

Natriello and his associates concluded the following about the effectiveness of Chapter I programs:

The severity of the learning deficits of disadvantaged students is such that their participation in the typical Chapter I program, for example, does no more than raise their performance to the top of the bottom quartile on tests in critical skills areas. The long-term consequences of such modest effects is that by the 10th grade one of two of these students will be a dropout and/or functionally illiterate. (p. 96)

Avoiding the Pitfalls of Pullout Programs

As an "Early School," Highland is a comprehensive program which avoids the programmatic pitfalls of all these compensatory education strategies, especially of the pullout variety. The first pitfall is a lack of coordination in instruction across boundaries between special and regular programs. The second is the loss of instructional time due to movement between special and regular programs. A third problem of traditional compensatory education programs is the loss of feeling of responsibility for the ED students by regular teachers, who too often then stigmatize them as inferior to regular students. In short, a pullout program can be very disruptive in a teacher-centered classroom, both to those pulled out and to those left in class.

If all students were thought of as needing individualized attention, however, instruction could be redesigned to accommodate everyone in the class without disruption. Highland's Montessori-style multigraded settings allow free movement, individualized pacing, small group work, cooperative learning, peer tutoring, even idiosyncratic academic activities, as well as remediation that does not call attention to itself.

Compensatory education funds would have to be shifted from

paying for extra teachers to work with the pullout students to paying early childhood teachers to work with three-, four-, and five-year-olds. Startup costs for materials, training, and other expenses could be split between federal and private funds.

Think Beyond the Early School Concept

Some educators concerned about educationally disadvantaged children have been thinking even beyond the Early School concept. For example, Massachusetts' successful Brookline Early Education Project (BEEP) included a program for infants and toddlers and a heavy emphasis on child health and nutrition. It was supported for nine years by private funds. Highland people are thinking about these kinds of necessary changes as well. One Highland teacher expressed her wish to buy the large house next door in order to create an infants and toddlers program for Highland which would emphasize many of the elements BEEP established.

Conclusion

Highland Community School is not a perfect template to which other schools must be fitted, because its circumstances are unique. But in doing a lot of things right, it speaks powerfully to other schools about how they might educate their students more effectively.

Highland's "frontal assault on every aspect of [traditional] schooling" has been to rethink how a school is to be organized and must function. Its value-base, its sense of purpose, and its dependence on parents and other community members have created a strong web woven together by its augmented Montessori curriculum and its six-year span of instruction. Highland Community School *is* a community, a gem becoming increasingly precious in our modern world for its increasing rarity. Yet by that very fact, I believe it is a beacon of hope to public education.

References

Ascher, Carol. 1992. School programs for African American males . . . and females. *Phi Delta Kappan* 73 (June): 777–82.

Barth, Roland. 1990. *Improving Schools from Within: Teachers, Parents, and Principals Can Make the Difference*. San Francisco: Jossey-Bass.

Bellah, Robert N., Richard Madsen, William Sullivan, Ann Swidler, and Steven M. Tipton. 1985. *Habits of the Heart: Individualism and Commitment in American Life*. Berkeley and Los Angeles, CA: University of California Press.

Benson, Laura. 1994. Urban education: Reform at Henry Park Elementary. Unpublished report available from the author of this book.

Billingsly, Andrew. 1992. *Climbing Jacob's Ladder: The Enduring Legacy of African-American Families*. New York: Simon & Schuster.

Brandt, Ron. 1992. On building learning communities: A conversation with Hank Levin. *Educational Leadership* 50 (September): 19–23.

Breitborde, Lawrence. 1993. Multiculturalism and cultural relativism after the commemoration [of the 500th Anniversary of Columbus discovering America]. *Social Education* 57 (March): 104–8.

Brophy, J., and J. Choquette. 1973. *Divergent production in Montessori children*. Paper presented at the biennial meeting of the Society for Research in Child Development, Philadelphia. ED 080 212.

Bryk, Anthony S., Valerie E. Lee, and Peter B. Holland. 1993. *Catholic Schools and the Common Good*. Cambridge, MA: Harvard University Press.

Chattin-McNichols, John. 1992. What does research say about Montessori?" In *Montessori in Contemporary American Culture*, Margaret Howard Loeffler, ed. Portsmouth, NH: Heineman, pp. 69–100.

Cicirelli, Victor G. 1969. *The Impact of Head Start: An Evaluation of the Effects of Head Start on Children's Cognitive and Affective Development*. Athens, Ohio: Ohio University, and New York: Westinghouse Learning Corporation.

Clark, Reginald. 1983. *Family Life and School Achievement: Why Poor Children Succeed or Fail*. Chicago: University of Chicago Press.

Comer, James. 1980. *School Power: Implications of an Intervention Project*. New York: Free Press.

———. 1985. Empowering black children's educational environments. In *Black Children: Social, Educational, and Parental Environments*, Harriet P. McAdoo and John. L. McAdoo, eds. Beverly Hills, CA: Sage.

———. 1988a. *Maggie's American Dream: The Life and Times of a Black Family*. New York: Plume.

———. 1988b. A social skills curriculum. *New York Times* Education Supplement (February 7): 27–31.

———. 1988c. Educating poor minority children. *Scientific American* 259 (November): 42–48.

Corley, Daniel. 1989. Lessons of an inner-city independent school, *Education Week* (October 11): 22.

Cotton, Kathleen. 1991. Community collaboration to improve the quality of life for urban youth and their families. Portland, OR: Northwest Regional Educational Laboratory Newsletter (July 6–7).

Cremin, Lawrence A. 1988. *American Education: The Metropolitan Experience.* New York: Harper & Row.

David, Jane L. 1994. School-based decision making: Kentucky's test of decentralization. *Phi Delta Kappan* (May): 706–12.

Demographics of Highland Community School Service Area. 1992. A report prepared by Milwaukee Associates in Urban Development Neighborhood Data Center, Milwaukee, Wisconsin.

Derman-Sparks, Louise, and the ABC Task Force. 1989. *Anti-Bias Curriculum: Tools for Empowering Young Children.* Washington, DC: NAEYC.

Drug abuse among blacks. 1990. Monograph available from Northwest Regional Educational Laboratory Newsletter. Portland, OR.

Duck, Lloyd. 1981. *Teaching with Charisma.* Boston: Allyn and Bacon.

Effective schooling practices: A research synthesis 1990 update. 1990. Unsigned monograph available from Northwest Regional Educational Laboratory, 101 SW Main St., Portland, OR.

Fiske, Edward B. 1991. *Smart Schools, Smart Kids.* New York: Simon & Schuster.

Foren, John. 1994. Top educator balks at Michigan's first charter school. *Grand Rapids Press.* (September 21): 1B.

Fromm, Erich. 1956. *The Art of Loving.* New York: Harper & Row.

Gardner, Howard. 1991. *The Unschooled Mind: How Children Think and How Schools Should Teach.* New York: Basic Books.

Haglund, Rick. 1992. "Go, go" stress of juggling job, family roles becomes commonplace. *Grand Rapids Press* (February 16): 3D.

Hainstock, Elizabeth. 1986. *The Essential Montessori.* Updated Edition. New York: Penguin Books.

Hauser-Cram, Penny, Donald E. Pierson, Deborah Klein Walker, and Terrence Tivnan. 1991. *Early Education in the Public Schools: Lessons from a Comprehensive Birth-to-Kindergarten Program.* San Francisco, CA: Jossey-Bass.

Havighurst, Robert J. 1979. Local community participation in educational policy making and school administration. In *Community Participation in Education,* Carl Grant, ed. Boston: Allyn and Bacon, pp. 22–24.

Heath, Shirley Brice, and Milbrey W. McLaughlin, eds. 1993. *Identity and Inner-City Youth: Beyond Ethnicity and Gender.* New York: Teachers College Press.

Herzog, Karen. 1993. Parents part of process at Highland. *Milwaukee Sentinel* (October 16): 5A.

Hewlett, Sylvia A. 1991. *When the Bough Breaks: The Cost of Neglecting Our Children.* New York: Basic Books.

Hojnacki, William P. 1979. What is a neighborhood? *Social Policy* (September–October): 47–52.

Johnson, Charles. 1992. Reinventing Africa. *New York Times Book Review* (June 21): 8.

Joyce, Bruce, Richard Hersh, and Michael McKibbin. 1983. *The Structure of School Improvement.* New York: Longman.

Kahn, David. 1992. A response to Lilian Katz's questions for Montessorians. In *Montessori in Contemporary American Culture,* Margaret Howard Loeffler, ed. Portsmouth, NH: Heineman, 195–201.

Kendall, Frances. 1983. *Diversity in the Classroom: A Multicultural Approach to the Education of Young Children.* New York: Teachers College Press.

Kidder, John Tracy. 1989. *Among Schoolchildren.* New York: Avon.

King, Martin Luther, Jr. 1963. *Strength to Love.* New York: Pocket Books.

Kleg, Milton. 1993. On the NCSS [National Council for the Social Studies] curriculum guidelines for multicultural education. *Social Education* 57 (February): 58–9.

Klimes-Dougan, Bonnie, Jose A. Lopez, Perry Nelson, and Howard S. Adelman. 1992. Two studies of low income parents' involvement in schooling. *The Urban Review* 24 (3): 185–202.

Kolata, Gina. 1992. More children are employed, often perilously. *New York Times.* (June 21): 14.

Lamb, Curt. 1975. *Political Power in Poor Neighborhoods.* New York: Schenkman.

Lareau, Annette. 1989. *Home Advantage: Social Class and Parental Intervention in Elementary Education.* New York: Falmer.

Lemann, Nicholas. 1991. *The Promised Land: The Great Black Migration and How It Changed America.* New York: Knopf.

Miller, L., and L. Dyer. 1975. Four preschool programs: Their dimensions and effects. *Monographs of the Society for Research in Child Development* (162).

Minsky, Marvin. 1985. *The Society of Mind.* New York: Basic Books.

Montessori, Maria. 1964. *The Montessori Method.* New York: Schocken.

———. 1967. *The Absorbent Mind.* New York: Dell.

Natriello, Gary, Edward McDill, and Aaron Pallas. 1990. *Schooling Disadvantaged Children: Racing Against Catastrophe.* New York: Teachers College Press.

The new face of America. 1993. *Time,* Special Issue (Fall): 15.

Ogbu, John. 1974. *The Next Generation: An Ethnography of Education in an Urban Neighborhood.* New York: Academic Press.

Olsen, Laurie, and Nina Mullen. 1991. Embracing diversity: California teachers are finding new ways to bridge cultural chasms. *Equity and Choice* (Spring): 5–17.

Orr, Eleanor Wilson. 1987. *Twice as Less: Black English and the Performance of Black Students in Mathematics and Science.* New York: Norton.

Oxley, Diana. 1994. Organizing schools into small units: Alternatives to homogeneous grouping. *Phi Delta Kappan* (March): 521–6.

Perkinson, Henry J. 1991. *The Imperfect Panacea: American Faith in Education, 1865–1990.* Third Edition. New York: McGraw-Hill.

Purkey, Stewart, and Marshall Smith. 1983. Effective schools: A review. *Elementary School Journal* 83(4): 427–53.

Richardson, Virginia, Ursula Casanova, Peggy Placier, and Karen Guilfoyle. 1989. *School Children at Risk.* New York: Falmer (Taylor and Francis).

Rogers, David, and Norman H. Chung. 1983. *110 Livingston Street Revisited: Decentralization in Action.* New York: New York University Press.

Rubin, Lillian. 1976. *Worlds of Pain: Life in the Working-Class Family.* New York: Basic Books.

Sameroff, Arnold, and Susan C. McDonough. 1994. Educational implications of developmental transitions: Revisiting the 5- to 7-year shift. *Phi Delta Kappan* (November): 188–93.

Sarasohn, David. 1992. French commitment to early education is example to U.S. *Grand Rapids Press* (August 16): 19A.

Schlechty, Phillip, and Robert Cole. 1993. Why not charter school boards? *American School Board Journal* (November).

Schmidt, Fran, and Alice Friedman. 1991. *Creative Conflict Solving for Kids, Grades 3–4.* Miami Beach, FL: Grace Contrino Abrams Peace Education Foundation, Inc., P.O. Box 191153, Miami Beach, FL 33119.

Schneider, Barbara J., and James S. Coleman. 1993. *Parents, Their Children, and Schools.* Boulder, CO: Westview Press.

Sergiovanni, Thomas J. 1994. *Building Community in Schools.* San Francisco, CA: Jossey-Bass.

Shanker, Albert. 1994a. A balance of power. *New York Times* (February 20): 6E.

———. 1994b. First things first. *New York Times* (November 13): 7E.

Sizer, Theodore R. 1992. *Horace's School: Redesigning the American High School.* Boston: Houghton Mifflin.

Slavin, Robert E., Nancy L. Karweit, and Barbara A. Wasik, eds. 1994a. *Preventing Early School Failure: Research, Policy, and Practice.* Boston: Allyn and Bacon.

Slavin, Robert E., Nancy A. Madden, Lawrence J. Dolan, Barbara A. Wasik, and Steven M. Ross. 1994b. Whenever and wherever we choose: The replication of "Success For All." *Phi Delta Kappan* 75 (April): 639–47.

Sleeter, Christine. 1993. Multicultural education: Five views. *Education Digest* (March): 53–7.

Snow, Catherine E., Wendy S. Barnes, Jean Chandler, Irene F. Goodman, and Lowry Hemphill. 1991. *Unfulfilled Expectations: Home and School Influences on Literacy.* Cambridge, MA: Harvard University Press.

Statistical Abstract of the United States: 1995, 115th Edition. 1996. Washington, DC: U.S. Bureau of the Census.

Study traces best scores in tests to small schools. 1994. *New York Times* (September 21): 13.

Summerfield, Harry. 1971. *The Neighborhood-Based Politics of Education.* Columbus, OH: Charles Merrill.

Sylvester, Paul Skilton. 1994. Elementary school curricula and urban transformation. *Harvard Educational Review* 64 (Fall): 309–31.

Tatum, Beverly. 1992. Learning about racism. *Harvard Educational Review* 62 (Spring): 1–24.

Turner, Joy Starry. 1992. Montessori's writings versus Montessori's practices. In *Montessori in Contemporary American Culture,* Margaret Howard Loeffler, ed. Portsmouth, NH: Heineman, pp. 17–47.

Vann, Sonya. 1992. In the African tradition, children learn the meaning of heritage and adulthood. *Grand Rapids Press* (July 8): 3B.

Walberg, Herbert J., and Richard P. Niemiec. 1994. Is Chicago school reform working? *Phi Delta Kappan* (May): 713–715.

Washington, Valora, and Ura Jean Oyemade. 1987. *Project Head Start: Past, Present, and Future Trends in the Context of Family Needs.* New York: Garland.

Webb, Rodman, and Robert Sherman. 1990. *Schooling and Society,* Second Edition. New York: Macmillan.

West, Cornel. 1993. *Race Matters.* Boston: Beacon Press.

Why Do Some Urban Schools Succeed: The Phi Delta Kappa Study of Exceptional Urban Elementary Schools. 1980. Bloomington, IN: Phi Delta Kappa.

Williams, Michael R. 1985. *Neighborhood Organizations: Seeds of a New Urban Life.* Westport, CT: Greenwood.

———. 1989. *Neighborhood Organizing for Urban School Reform.* New York: Teachers College Press.

Wilson, William J. 1991. *The Truly Disadvantaged.* Chicago: University of Chicago Press.

Wright, John W., general editor. 1995. *The Universal Almanac 1996.* Kansas City, MO: Andrews and McMeel.

Wynne, Edward, and Herbert Walberg. 1994. Persisting groups: An overlooked force for learning. *Phi Delta Kappan* (March): 527–30.

Zeldin, Shepherd. 1991. A matter of faith: The interpersonal aspects of restructuring in a "Comer" school. *Equity and Choice* 7 (Spring): 52–57.

Zigler, Edward, and Susan Meunchow. 1992. *Head Start: The Inside Story of America's Most Successful Educational Experiment.* New York: Basic Books.

Index

About the Author

Michael R. Williams is Professor-in-the-College at Aquinas College, Grand Rapids, Michigan. He has taught undergraduate and graduate courses in education, general studies, philosophy, and urban studies. He received the Licentiate in Philosophy from St. Louis University in 1966, the Master of Science in Mechanical Engineering from Marquette University in 1970, and the PhD in Urban Education from the University of Wisconsin-Milwaukee. After teaching in the Milwaukee Public School System, he cofounded and was the first administrator of the Highland Community School of Milwaukee. He is the author of *Neighborhood Organizations: Seeds of a New Urban Life* (Greenwood Press, 1985) and *Neighborhood Organizing for Urban School Reform* (Teachers College Press, 1989).